UNCLE

A "JERRIATRIC" LOVE STORY

GARY W. GORSUCH

gorsuchBOOKS

4009 SW Halcyon Road
Tualatin, Oregon 97062

ISBN-13: 978-1478388043
ISBN-10: 1478388048

CONTENTS

ACKNOWLEDGEMENTS

Thank you, Bob Hicks, for your encouragement to get my thoughts out of my head onto paper.

A special thanks to Sherie Sherrill and Jennifer Hansen, for the spit and polish that makes this book something more than what otherwise only a mother would read.

A very special thank you to my darling daughters, Cathi and Berniece. They willingly made adjustments and sacrifices in their teen years that went well beyond what could be considered natural and normal.

Most of all, I thank Judi, the love of my life, for your willingness, the sacrifices and all the assistance you've given that made Uncle's sojourn with our family possible.

PREFACE

People can go through life in one of two ways, (1.) They can simply "muddle through," reacting to ever-changing circumstances with no well-defined purpose and no real plan to provide either for their own futures or those of their loved ones; or (2.) They can carefully plan and faithfully execute that plan so that, rather than react to surprises, they respond to conditions they expected and for which they prepared. Of course, these two approaches are extremes; most of us find ourselves somewhere in between. Even if I were the most ardent #2 (and I'm not), it would have been impossible to plan and prepare for Uncle's coming to live with us. A lot of circumstances beyond our control or wildest imaginations led to my mother's ninety-six-year-old Uncle becoming an integral part of our family and my business. Our lives were irrevocable changed.

We moved to Portland, Oregon, from Gridley, California, in October of 1970. The move put us conveniently right between my wife's family in Central California and my own family in Northwestern Washington. With very little money in our pockets and a house yet unsold in Gridley, but also with the courage of the young and innocent, we bundled up five-year-old Cathi and four-year-old Berniece, crammed a few survival provisions into our red, fastback, two-door Ford Fairlane, stored the rest of our possessions, and headed north.

Upon arriving at our destination – Portland, Oregon – we went to the home of the only person there we knew, Uncle Charlie, then a mere eighty-seven years old. He welcomed us with characteristically open arms, insisting that we stay with him until we could find our own place to live. The very next day we found temporary but suitable quarters, thanked Uncle, and with the two cots that he insisted we take with us, set up our own housekeeping.

1

ONLY A MEDIOCRE PERSON IS ALWAYS AT HIS BEST

Deep down, I knew it was to be our last trip together. But then I suppose if I really had thought that, I would have bathed, clipped and cleaned out under his fingernails and the nails of the one foot that still had toes on it. He'd lost the front fourth of his left foot back in the early 1900's in one of his many near-fatal accidents. However, even if I had consciously known Uncle's time was within days of being up, I'd still have rationalized countless reasons why death could never claim him, at least in my lifetime. Charles Neilson Ono had come into this world (in Larvick, Norway) on the 1883rd year of his Lord, on May 7th. He was called "Uncle Charlie" by almost everyone in my generation and just "Uncle" by those of us who knew and loved him best. He was 61 ½ years my senior, and at age 37 I'm considered old by my own offspring. Uncle goes back as far as I can pull anything out of my gray computer, and until the closing few days after our last ride together, he had always looked the same – wrinkle free round face with equally round wire-rimmed glasses, a few wisps of white hair, a stout body once over six feet tall but now shrunk and slightly stooped to just under five-seven, and skin smooth enough to make a baby jealous. But all of these physical details would pale to insignificance against the array of hats and caps he'd wear, the last of which was the pancake variety with a little short bill. He was seldom without it, even when he slept.

That day, I helped Uncle out to our trusty 1978 beige and brown Plymouth Volare, mostly carrying him, as I had ended up having to do these last few weeks. "I can't make it," he'd groan.

"Oh, sure, you can, Uncle. You just need a little help."

I'd haul him to his feet, rotate him one-half turn, loop my arms under his and around his middle, and clasp my hands together across his chest. I'd then back out the door with a ca-thump as his black leather Red Wing boots, always in need of a little polish, bounced over the threshold. We'd continue backing towards the car with Uncle's boot heels digging into the gravel of our driveway, leaving a trail of neat little parallel trenches, with the cane clutched in his hand bouncing an occasional stone or two out of place. Not too long before, I had taken Uncle to the Red Wing store in the Fred Meyer shopping center just off McLoughlin Blvd. His ancient hook-and-eye, high-top shoes had finally become unmanageable. Besides having been resoled three too many times, Uncle's condition had gotten to the point that he would spend half the morning getting into his shoes, and even then the job still wasn't done right. Uncle really enjoyed his new boots. His appreciation was expressed more than once with such words as, "These boots are one of the best things that's ever happened to me! Boy, oh boy, do I love these boots." Ruth and Esther, Uncle's second cousins, though extremely generous to Uncle in dozens of other ways, thought that the fifty dollars we paid was a bit steep, but Uncle would have gladly given five hundred.

"Feel all right?" I'd ask, settling him into his side of the front seat.

"Certainly, I couldn't feel better," would come his usual answer.

The facts of the matter were that he could have felt much better, especially in his groin and genital area. Uncle had had problems holding his urine ever since he'd had his prostate gland reamed out. He leaked on a regular basis, and since he pretty much smelled the same way all the time, and his smeller was nearly worn out, he didn't seem to notice. But I knew there had to be some sort of device to help with this noisome problem. I went to a drug store and, try as I might for the only male clerk in the store, I ended up with the youngest, most self-conscious female to ever hold such a position. Of course, I wasn't much help in trying to explain my problem tactfully—I mean Uncle's problem, though I'm sure she thought it must be mine. Many red-faced hours later (though it actually only took minutes) it dawned on her the type of device I wanted. She quickly handed me a manufacturer's booklet full of all sorts of mechanical health-aid products and told me to take it home, read it over, and then bring it back. "And he'll," she pointed at the only male working in the store, "order it for you." I did, he did, and Uncle got a condom catheter. I called it his "pecker pouch," and he called it his "penis harness."

The first time, I put it on too tightly and he swelled right up. Uncle took one look and said, "Boy, oh boy, it's been years since it has been that big!" Unfortunately, this time I had unwittingly placed his condom catheter in such a way that the circulation had been restricted to the scrotum and penis, causing infection to set in. Uncle hadn't complained, and when I finally discovered the problem, the harness had been on in that position for several days. I took the gadget off him and tried his various ointments and salves but, seeing that the problem was going to require something more than one of these wonder remedies, I called Dr. Morita, our family practitioner. He was his usual non-threatening, gentle self and more than understanding. He should have chewed me out for not keeping a closer eye on the device. He asked a number of questions and finally recommended that I come in later that day so he could take a good look at the problem. With that, he turned me over to Jeanine, his office nurse, a friend of my wife, who arranged to squeeze Uncle into their already busy schedule. The appointment was set for 2 p.m. that same afternoon. By this time, half the morning was gone, and when I asked Uncle if he wanted to stay home and rest until his doctor's appointment or go out for one call to Gervis, Uncle quickly said, his voice alive with anticipation, "Where you go, I'll go."

At this point, I'm reminded of the ancient story of Ruth, the Moabitess. She had married a foreigner who had moved into Moab, her homeland, with his parents and brother. Now her husband, father-in-law, and brother-in-law had all died. The woman who had married her husband's brother (also a Moabitess) had decided to return to her own household. Naomi, Ruth's mother-in-law, urged Ruth to do the same. Naomi had decided to go back to her own land, Israel, in utter poverty, and felt she had no right to ask her daughter-in-law to come with her. Ruth, however, felt differently and said, "Don't urge me to leave you or to turn back from you. WHERE YOU GO, I WILL GO; AND WHERE YOU STAY, I WILL STAY. Your people will be my people and your God my God." Many times during the two years that Uncle and I lived and traveled together, he said to me, and many

4

others, these famous words of Ruth with just one slight alteration, "Where Jerry goes, I go!" He never got the name right, (my name is Gary), but with such words of love and loyalty, who'd care!

So here we are now - I've got Uncle into the car. All went well - he sat down, grimacing in pain until his private parts situated themselves into the new position he had taken. We went past the mid-point of our driveway, under the Douglas fir tree that hung at a precipitous angle over the driveway. Almost daily Uncle had told me, "Jerry, if you had any sense you'd have cut that tree down long ago." We took a right turn onto Kruger Road, past the mailbox that had just recently been returned to us. Our neighborhood pranksters find no greater pleasure than smashing (or in our case, uprooting) the box, post and all, and dumping it five miles away in the Sherwood Shopping Center parking lot. Fortunately for us, the battered box had been clearly marked and a local, conscientious, off-duty postal employee spotted it, scooped it up, and brought it to the Post Office. They in turn sent out a card telling me to come and pick up my mailbox. I felt rather funny, as I stood in line with stamp-buyers and package fetchers, picking up at my turn my mailbox, mud-encrusted post and all. With a snicker or two from the postal patrons behind and alongside me, Dave Nichols, our Sherwood postmaster (whom I've yet to let forget the day he accidentally flew the flag upside down, a crime I believe punishable by death or something worse for one in his position), said, "Jerry, you'd better let Uncle plant your postal box this time. Then it won't be so easy for our local juvenile delinquents to pull it out."

2

IF YOU DO SOMETHING WRONG AT LEAST ENJOY IT

The day was sunny with just a few small white fluffy clouds fleeting lazily in an otherwise clear sky. I punched the radio button to get my favorite 24-hour news station, KYXL. A major disaster would be just the thing to cheer Uncle up. Whether natural or otherwise, Uncle seemed to love disasters. The bloodier, the more heart-rending, the higher the body count, the more enthusiastic Uncle became. An event would really need to be something out of the ordinary to gain and keep his undivided attention. I can still see Uncle sitting with this nose almost pressed up against one of our plate glass picture windows during the height of an electrical storm. He gleefully rubbed his hands with each clap of thunder, smiled and twinkled his eyes at each flash of lightening, saying "Boy, oh boy!"

Uncle didn't march to the beat of another drummer; nobody has ever played the cadence he marched to, or ever will. He was the King of Eccentrics, living as he pleased yet controlled by a value system that most of the time bordered on Sainthood. King Solomon wrote in Proverbs 13:7, "There is he that maketh himself rich yet hath nothing, there is he that maketh himself poor, yet hath riches." Uncle gave all the appearances of wealth. His dress, his demeanor, his extravagant spending, his generosity to any who came to him with either real or contrived need, his expensive taste in food and drink, his love of travel – all of that belied the fact that Uncle was really quite poor. Yet as Solomon, the worlds' all-time richest man said, ". . . he that maketh himself poor, yet hath riches." Uncle was the richest man I've ever known.

Uncle usually was as honest as the day is long, yet at times that honesty had a perverted "eye for an eye, tooth for a tooth" (and in one particular case, "cord for a cord") twist. After hearing about someone stealing a couple of cords of wood he'd watched me cut up and leave in my friends' forest to dry, he couldn't forget the theft and must have been thinking of some way to make it right. Not many days later, as we were driving a back road between Scholls and Hillsboro on our way to Tillamook, he spotted a large stack of wood and said, "Stop! Let's take that wood! Someone took ours, so we have the right to take someone else's." This skewed philosophy didn't just manifest itself in his golden years, either. Uncle told me about the time he'd been persuaded against his will to reload some shotgun shells for an older, demanding brother. In the process, to get back at his brother for making him do something he didn't want to, Uncle doubled up on the powder. When Big Brother discharged his gun with the "special" reloads, Uncle chortled, "It knocked him right on his butt."

"Don't lie to me, Charlie," his brother had growled. "How much powder did you put in those shells?"

As long as I'm on a few of Uncle's paradoxical virtues, I might mention his attitude towards litter. Uncle didn't feel that "every litter bit hurts;" rather, "A little litter don't hurt." In fact, his little was often a lot. He complained when Judi and the girls picked up around the house, especially when they got near his territory. He called their efforts a waste of good time. His unconcern about litter went beyond merely kicking off his shoes and socks and letting them lie. He would actually spit seeds, hulls, or whatever onto the floor, whether in the car, at home, or in the church. If a food item had paper on it, he'd throw that and whatever he didn't eat out the window, providing I didn't grab it first. Several times, forgetting that we were driving down the freeway at sixty miles per hour, he almost literally littered himself all over the highway. He'd unlock and open the door, thinking we were home and it was time to get out.

Uncle loved my daughters and thought I was a bit too permissive, even with my neo-Victorian ideas and demands that I always know where they are and whom they're with. I guess he felt I should never let them out of my sight.

"You mean you let them go to town all by themselves? Don't you know there's lots of crazy people out there?" he'd demand.

He fretted and stewed, finally resolving his frustration by saying that he'd make each one of the girls (Berniece, 15, and Cathi, 16) a club out of a stack of his old lead fishing sinkers. That seemed to satisfy him, and from that point on he never said any more about the girls going off to town by themselves. And no, he never made them clubs from any of his old lead fishing sinkers.

Not only did Uncle love my daughters and most other people, but he also loved animals. He'd often reach down and pick up one of our little dogs saying, "The poor tings, the poor tings . . .," stroking them until they, or he, or sometimes both, fell asleep. Finally, I gave him a black dog, the last of a litter that hadn't been taken by anyone. I asked him what he'd name it, and without wasting a minute he said, Caesar. So Caesar it was, with the only problem being that Uncle couldn't remember what he'd named it. Well, at least not exactly. He'd call it Nero, Julius, and every now and then with a little assistance, Caesar. He really loved that little dog, but not quite as much as I had originally thought. I got a black, 175-pound Great Dane to fend off prowlers and discourage burglars. I was as proud as could be of that dog and was anxious to get Uncle's reaction to him. Right after the folks we got him from dropped him off, I brought him in and introduced him to Uncle. He took one look, began stroking Boris the VIII on the head, and then said, "Jerry, do you suppose I could trade in my little black dog for a Saint Bernard? I've always wanted one."

3

YOU OUGHT TO HAVE SEEN THE ONES THAT GOT AWAY

Down Kruger Road we went, winding our way through Chehalem Mountain's rolling hills and gullies. The branches and leaves of a myriad of trees hung over our country road, often completely blocking out the sun. I subconsciously noted mailbox names. First the Gerlach's who've helped me with many of the projects on our place. The one we've enjoyed the most is our little trout pond. I worked days and weeks trying to clean out the area on either side of the creek in the gully I'd selected for the pond. At just the right time, when there was the proper amount of moisture in the soil for ideal compaction, Norm Gerlach brought over his small but rugged cat. We worked for hours just yarding out old dead and down, water-logged material that was impossible to burn, and dispose of in place. Finally, after many days, buckets of sweat, and all the strains, bumps, scrapes, and scratches that go along with this type of work, the pond with its earthen dam stood complete. It reached from the slope that would soon extend into the water to the slope on the other side spanning over forty feet. The top part of the dam had been leveled and was about twelve feet across. The earth in and around where the water soon would be lay barren and bleak. It would be months before the vegetation would reemerge to create the natural foliage of fern and other native plants that we now enjoy. If I'd known ahead of time how much work it was to take, I'd never have tackled it. However, with further additions in the weeks that followed – a culvert spillway, a by-pass ditch, and rock work for bank support – the pond was ready to be filled. I plugged off the 4-inch galvanized pipe I'd gotten from Rudy up the road, and in about 2 ½ days the pond filled, ready for some fish. Uncle had been kept posted as to the progress, and once in a while he would take a peek just to make sure we were doing everything right.

When I told Uncle that soon we'd go to a private trout farm that I'd located and buy some rainbow fingerling trout, he snorted, "You might as well burn the money! You'll never get them here alive."

He was so genuinely convinced that I was caught off-guard. "What do you mean, Uncle? I'll use a garbage can lined with a big plastic bag and just drive them over here from the trout farm."

"The government couldn't do it, so there is no vay in the vorld that you will be able to get them over here alive. They'll all die first."

With careful further questioning, I soon found that Uncle had read a newspaper article about an attempted fish transplant project by the State Fish and Game Commission that had gone awry, almost all the fish dying. He never said a word about the hundreds of successful fish-planting projects he'd read or heard about. He just went on and on like a nagging wife how my attempt would fail miserably, resulting in the death of "every last one." By this time, though, I was inwardly shaken, not sure anymore that I could pull it off, but I tentatively rose to the challenge to prove by any means that I could bring back live fish.

"Do you want to go along, Uncle?" I said, thinking that if he didn't I'd somehow have to figure out a way to talk him into it. But with the eager anticipation of an opportunity for an "I told you so," Uncle jumped at my offer. Just before leaving, however, I rounded up a tire pump. Then we were off to the Woodburn Trout Farm. I'd phoned ahead so they were expecting us, and it wasn't long until we'd picked up our 500 fish and some feed and were heading the twenty miles home. The garbage can was stuffed in the trunk, holding the trunk lid open but tied securely down. Every five miles or so, though I was told it wouldn't be necessary, I stopped the car, grabbed the tire plump, (I wasn't going to take any chances!), took the cover off the can, and pumped extra air into the water.

"You can't do it," Uncle kept insisting. "They'll all die," he repeated over and over again, until finally we had arrived home. I stopped the car, jumped out, and fearfully peered between the lip and the cover of the can as I carefully lifted it off.

"They're alive!" I shouted triumphantly to Uncle.

"You're crazy," grumped Uncle. "They can't be. The government couldn't do it, so how can you?"

I raced to the house and grabbed a plastic bucket that I'd use to transfer the fish into the pond. I dipped up a bucketful, and with water still dripping off the sides and bottom, dangled it inches from Uncle's nose.

"I can't believe it," admitted Uncle. "The government couldn't do it, but you did. I just can't believe it."

Over the next year and several months before Uncle died, whenever I caught a fish I'd make sure Uncle saw it. His reaction was always the same.

"Remember those fish you said would die, Uncle? Well, look at them."

"Yeah," he'd say. "Just can't believe it. The government sure couldn't do it."

The miracle trout grew from 1 ½ inch fingerlings to fish as long as 17 or 18 inches, and Uncle enjoyed eating quite a number of them.

On past the Gerlach's. We waved to Paul Cappoen who was out working in his field. He's been doing a lot more of this lately, since he was fired by his hellfire-and-damnation former employer. He said bachelor Paul used too much foul language on the job. He knew nothing of Paul's unselfish care and concern for the 80-year-old widow next door, who received everything from regular trips to the grocery store to free maintenance on her home – charity I'm sure Paul's sanctimonious former employer himself couldn't have been bothered with. We picked up the widow lady and her granddaughter, Kelly, many Sunday mornings, and I flushed in shame when I thought of the Christianity Paul's former employer overtly espoused. Florence was the lady's name, and she thought both Uncle and Paul were very special. Uncle enjoyed the attention she gave him but always remained a bit aloof. I think the reason for his coolness came out one Sunday morning when we passed her place without stopping. She had called saying she had company and would not be going to church that morning, but I hadn't told Uncle.

"Aren't we going to pick up the OLD LADY?" asked Uncle.

"Old?" I said. "She's almost twenty years younger than you are!"

"Aw," said Uncle, and he mumbled and grumbled and then didn't say another word. Apparently Uncle considered himself a more able physical specimen and would just as soon not get too friendly with someone whom he considered more decrepit than he.

4

I'D RATHER QUIT THAN FIGHT

We continued down Kruger Road to Highway 99W and made a right turn toward Newberg. About this time, I pulled out my Dutch Master's Presidents, the five-pack variety, and there were only a couple left. I unwrapped one, placed it between my lips, and before lighting up, waited for the inevitable lecture on the evils of tobacco. I've heard it said that a bad habit is often replaced by something far worse. That describes Uncle perfectly. His far worse habit was the pride of having been able to give up his cigar chain-smoking. His pride came out in his downright malicious, almost antagonistic attitude toward any and all who'd not gained victory over tobacco's stranglehold. His own personal triumph was indeed colorful, but due mainly to the tremendous respect he had held for a certain member of the medical profession.

Sometime in the thirties, Uncle went to his doctor with a stiff neck. In the course of the doctor's history-taking, he asked Uncle if he smoked.

"Why, sure," said Uncle. "I buy them by the box, take two fistfuls each morning, and light up one right after the other."

"That's it," said the doctor. "You've got to quit right now!"

"Can't I at least finish these?" And Uncle opened his jacket to reveal a breast pocket busting at the seams with one of his fistfuls of White Owl cigars.

"No," roared the doctor. "In fact, put them right here on the desk."

Uncle reluctantly fished every last White Owl out of his pocket and regretfully placed them on top of the medical man's massive desk. With one quick swipe of his hand, the doctor rolled each and every last one of them into the top drawer of his desk.

"And I'll bet he smoked every one of them himself!" was Uncle's final comment.

"Didn't you ever get the urge to smoke again?" I once asked Uncle.

"Get the urge? Boy, oh boy, did I ever! It took over two years before I ever stopped craving them. But I've never smoked since. The guys I worked with kept on offering them to me blowing smoke in my direction, hoping to get me hooked again so they could bum them off me. I used to supply all those guys with their smokes, but never again."

"So it went, and so it also would have been if Uncle had directed his zeal against strong drink. But he liked it too much for that. He would have put every Christian Temperance Legion chapter in the Northwest out of business, if it was up to him. Once, as we stood in the waiting room of a posh restaurant waiting to be seated, Uncle spotted a middle-age, athletic-looking gentleman puffing on a cigarette. Before I could stop him, Uncle reached out with his cane and gave the guy a good rap on the shins.

"Come over here," he said in a rather gruff, abrupt tone. I braced myself, wishing there was some way I could spare the kindly-looking man Uncle's wrath. But for this poor guy, his time had finally arrived.

"Do you realize what you're doing to yourself?" Uncle began. "I'll bet you could check with your doctor, and he could tell you to the day when you're going to die."

On and on Uncle went, verbally slashing, cutting and bruising the guy in every possible way. Probably the worst part for him, however, was his wife's continual nodding in agreement to each and every one of Uncle's words. The couple who was with this dear man stood with their mouths at half mast, and I may have noticed the other guy trying, as inconspicuously as possible, to make sure that his own pack was out of sight well below the upper opening of his pocket. Finally, our names were called and we left the folks as quickly as possible, which wasn't too fast seeing that Uncle had had a couple of drinks and was a little unsteady on his feet.

We were almost to Springbrook Road when Uncle finished his anti-smoking lecture. I assured him that I only had a cigar once in a while and that I didn't inhale the smoke. His parting shot was, "That's how it starts with everybody. Before you know it, you'll have one hanging out of your mouth all the time." I'm glad it takes only one hand to write these lines, leaving the other free to massage the stiffness in my neck. I guess I'd better give up Dutch Masters Presidents.

5

ALL YOU EVER WANTED TO KNOW ABOUT SEX BUT WERE AFRAID TO ASK . . . UNCLE

We turned left on Springbrook Road, past the little winery, then stopped to turn left again. We were now on the St. Paul Road, zipping past the dairy I sold my very first tank to. I had been given the lead and was anxious to prove to Mike Adams, the owner of Elenbass Dairy Supply, that he had made the smartest move yet for the company he had purchased just 60 days earlier - hiring me. I must have made eight or ten calls and at least three times that many phone conversations with the home office before the sale was finally made. But I'm now convinced that sale was made for reasons other than all my efforts. That final day when the contract was signed, as I now have it figured, was simply a matter of perfect timing, at least from my standpoint. I arrived at the dairy not long after lunch. I'd punched the bell six times before the dairyman finally wrenched open the door. His clothing looked as if each piece had been thrown on in a hurry, his hair stood up in spikes, and he seemed to be anxious to conclude the whole transaction. I presented my bid with all the changes we'd discussed, and with little more than a grunt or two, he signed the contract, giving me a several-thousand-dollar check as down payment. I'd grabbed the check and the rest of my paperwork and in seconds was outside. I glanced over my shoulder, just in case he was watching me leave and I could give him a wave. He was nowhere in sight. I jumped into the car, had it started and turned in record time, wanting to get out of there just in case the dairyman had had second thoughts. The blood was pumping, my excitement was exhilarating, and I could hardly wait to telephone the home office and boast of my success. I hummed a little tune which gave me the idea to flip the radio on, and the nasal twang of a country twosome came over the air waves: " . . . a-a-a-a-afternoon delight, a-a-a-a-a-afternoon delight . . . " In a flash, I'd instantly put the sequence of events into place; to this day I'm convinced that only my timing had made my very first tank sale. I can almost hear the passionate plea of the farm wife, "I don't care what it takes, but get rid of whoever it is as fast as you can and get back in here to me."

We were well past that dairy now, and the memory of that first sale was fading fast. It does, however, trigger for me several stories with a sexual slant that, thanks to Uncle, I'll never be able to forget, like the time I swung into Uncle's house to pick up a few items that he needed for his stay with us but hadn't brought with him. I was poking around in the closet, trying to find a couple more pairs of suspenders, when my hand slid across a hard object carefully wrapped in a brown paper bag. Using the excuse that it might be useful, but really to satisfy my curiosity, I pulled it out and there, bigger than life, was the latest edition of the book All You Ever Wanted to Know about Sex, but Were Afraid to Ask.

Now, I wouldn't call Uncle a Dirty Old Man or a Soiled Senior Citizen, but there were some times when he would seem to be pretty

22

close. Once, before he'd come to live with us on a permanent basis, I dropped by his home unannounced to check on how he was doing. He was glad to see me and insisted I have a cup of coffee with him. We marched from the front door through the living room, to the dining room, past the large table . . . "Wait! What's this?" I said to myself. "Why, it's a snapshot of a woman in a bikini." I studied the picture more closely as Uncle, who'd been ahead of me, moved on into the kitchen. There he began drawing the water, turning the stove on, and fiddling with other chores connected with making coffee. In the snapshot I noted some familiar curtains and buildings, and with a little closer attention, I saw that the scantily clad woman was the divorcee next door. The picture had been taken from the shadows of Uncle's kitchen nook! Though Uncle was by no means a celibate, I'm pretty sure his sexual activities were confined to marriage. He didn't live like many sailors with a gal in every port, but he had been a sailor who had hit at least five or six of the seven seas. During that period of his life, he must have heard, seen and learned a lot. One of the things he learned was a song that he strictly forbade my daughters to sing in church. In part it went like this:

". . . She was such a beauty and I thought it was my duty

I woke up in the gutter and they threw me in the shutter

And I went and asked no reason why . . . "

He also loved to sing,

"Daisy, Daisy, give me your answer true I'm half crazy all for the love of you…"

Once he got started, we could count on him singing it over and over again, twenty or thirty times.

A customer once asked how I ended up taking Uncle Charlie with me everywhere I went. Wanting to make the account more exciting than the gradual evolution of Uncle's moving in with us and his subsequent place beside me in our '78 Volare, I jokingly told the actual story (with an embellished ending) of a pre-Uncle visit to a dairy South of Woodburn. The dairyman and his farm were typical in most ways but, in one particular area, different from any I'd called upon before or since. He had seven gorgeous daughters. In responding to Judi's inquiry as to how things had gone that day, I told her I hadn't sold any dairy equipment but I did visit a dairyman who had seven beautiful daughters. Lest I end up in the doghouse or worse, I quickly followed with, "But none of them was as good-looking as you, Dear – but two of them came mighty close!"

"From that day on," I told the by-now-suspicious customer, "Judi has seen to it that Uncle never leaves my side."

The truth of the matter is that rather than Uncle's constant presence keeping me from being accused of compromising situations, the opposite has occurred.

For example, once, after an especially trying day, Uncle was a bit more than confused when we finally got home. Judi met us with a big smile and, for Uncle, a hug and a kiss. He ate it up, savoring every portion of the loving, caring caresses.

After taking full advantage of this attention, Uncle looked up with brimming eyes and said, "Who are you?"

"Why I'm Judi, Gary's wife," she replied.

"Huh, is that so?" snorted Uncle. "Then who in the world are those other vomen Jerry's with all the time?"

Yes, I often had to cringe at Uncle's "way with words." I've sometimes wished he were a tape recorder and I could push the "erase" button. Some of his infamous oral responses were mercifully uttered in the privacy of our home; too many others hit the public airwaves.

My daughters' bedrooms adjoin the family room that Uncle had taken over. Uncle managed to embarrass them, too. Once, Berniece had a couple of her friends over for the night. They kept scampering in and out of her bedroom, right past Uncle, who was relaxed, but not sleeping, in his favorite chair. Finally, he'd had it with the giggling turmoil and let fly with what the whole scene suggested to him, "This place looks like a whorehouse, and I'm not going to stand for it!"

On another occasion, Uncle and Judi and the girls and I gathered around his bed, watching the TV. I finally got up and said, "Come on, Judi, let's go upstairs to bed." Uncle snapped back, "Oh, let her stay! She can sleep here beside me. I won't touch her; I've been in neutral for years."

One final tale, along the same line, and we'll continue down the road again with Uncle. Earlier I mentioned Uncle's pouch (urinary device), and the blessing and cursing it had been. Uncle had two elderly, unmarried second cousins who had been school teachers. They were as helpful relatives as anybody could ever wish for. They had looked after Uncle religiously for years until he came to live with us. Even after that, they continued to help in many ways. They had been the ones who financed Uncle's pouches, about four or five of them (I lost count), and that leads me into this next story. They are the sweetest and most concerned individuals you'd ever meet. They also had to be in on or at least aware of everything that happened to Uncle.

25

On a visit to their home soon after the first "pecker pouch" or "penis harness" purchase, right in the middle of our conversation, Uncle insisted that I take him to the bathroom and drain it. With very little encouragement from me, the four of us squeezed into the main floor bathroom to observe the placement and procedure for draining the device. Through open fly, over dropped shorts, I carefully explained each strap and buckle, each tube and fold, each valve and compartment. Surely no instructor had a more attentive pair of pupils. The examination was thorough, and with Uncle's encouragement made sure no flap was left unlifted or fold unfurled.

6

A DEERE BARGAIN

St. Paul, Oregon, a town rich with history and home of the area's biggest and best rodeo – and as far as I can figure out, it's the sleepy town's only recent claim to fame. Rodeo time, once a year, is the only time you see more than three or four people on the city's sidewalks, and that wasn't today. We lumbered through town, turning left without stopping at the amber blinking light. We wheeled past the well-manicured cemetery, down through the marshy pond area, where you usually see a couple of colorful fishermen leaning up against the little bridge railing drowning a few hapless worms. Finally, we climbed up past the last of the homes on city lots and into the countryside. We usually saw several tractors in this next stretch, plowing, planting or harvesting row crops, grain, grass seed, or hops.

Every time I see a tractor, I'm reminded of the coveting that overpowered me, causing me to dream of myself in the driver's seat and reveling in the personal pleasure of one of my own. The itch got so bad that I religiously would comb through the farm equipment section of the Oregonian, the Portland area's largest newspaper. It wasn't long until Uncle realized I was looking for something in particular. When he finally asked, I told him I wanted a tractor. From that point on, every time he caught me going through the newspaper, he'd ask if I'd spotted anything interesting. With the right questions, it wasn't long until Uncle had pretty well figured out what was normally available and how much I could expect to pay. "Any tractor," according to Uncle, "worth having will cost at least $2,000." And since he knew that sum was more than I could afford, he said, "You'll just have to do without."

"I'll keep looking anyway, Uncle, and just maybe I'd find something for a few hundred dollars."

"You're wasting your time. I wish I had $2,000. If I did, I'd buy one for you."

I thanked him profusely, saying his willingness to get me a tractor if he had the money was almost as good as if he did, accompanying those words with a loving squeeze. In the weeks that followed, I don't care for what reason I picked up a paper, Uncle always assumed I was looking for a tractor. I might have been checking to see where the Trailblazers were placed in the NBA standings, but Uncle would say, "Anything under $2,000?"

Finally, after several months, I'd pretty well given up and just happened to mention my dream to my friend, John Alto, who owns our local Sherwood Chevron gas station. He said that his father had a small old John Deere "L", still running, that might just fit my needs. I called his father and arranged to stop by and take a look at it. When I mentioned to Uncle what it was we were going to be looking at, and when he heard it actually ran, and that all the owner wanted was $400, he said (sight unseen), "let's buy it?!

Following the directions that I'd been given by John, on the appointed day Uncle and I drove onto the Alto Farm. The senior

Altos lived on the slope of a hill just east of Oregon's coastal town of Seaside. Their house is nestled in a heavily forested area in between two small meadows circled with cedar fence posts, silver with age, strung with rusty but tight barbed wire. We drove up to and were about to pass a garage about one hundred feet from the house when I first saw the tractor parked inside. It appeared nicer than I even had expected. I quickly pulled to the side of the driveway, turned off the motor, and jumped out, telling Uncle at the same time that it looked good and I'd be right back. I stood quietly drinking in every detail of the tractor I knew would soon be mine. The rear tires were just like the huge man-dwarfing monsters with herringbone, cleat-like treads you see in farm magazines. But these tires were only three and one-half feet high. The top part of the tires was covered by angel-wing fenders capped with a metal seat similar to those found on antique cycle-bar mowers. The seat was positioned in under a black four-spoked steering wheel. The back of the tractor was tied to the front with a frame of two round pipe-like runners, with the drive shaft extending from differential (right under the seat, between the two runners) to the motor. And, oh – the motor! It was the classic two-cylindered John Deere that sounded like a heart which continuously missed every other beat. The motor and its few simple shrouds were anchored to the front frame above matching mag-like sculptured rims. The rims in turn were fitted with slender tires made with center and side rubber ribs running the full circumference of the face of the tire.

Mr. Alto had seen us drive up, but I had been so absorbed in the examination of the tractor that when he walked in on me from the house, his appearance startled me. I soon regained my composure, handled the introductions, and got right down to the business at hand. Mr. Alto started the tractor with a single crank and suggested I give it a thorough test drive. With the rhythmic "Ca-thump, ca-thump," I backed out of the garage, put it into gear, and drove up the drive past the house, through the gate into the farm meadow. After several minutes, I finally turned to drive back to where I'd left Uncle and the car. By this time Uncle had gotten out. From his position leaning against the car, he had been following me and my test run as best his dimming eyesight would allow. I pulled up within a few feet of Uncle. Leaning heavily on his cane, he hobbled the few feet to where the tractor stood idling and with real enthusiasm proclaimed, "Buy it!" Then, tears suddenly dripping down his cheeks, he mumbled, "God bless this tractor." I paid the man and drove off, trying to swallow the lump in my throat, just like the one I feel now as I write this recollection of that day.

7

JUST ONE MORE FOR THE ROAD

I t's an open, straight road for the next few miles, and then we take a hard right out across table-top smooth farmland. We sail through a couple of depressions in the otherwise flat landscape, negotiate two gentle S turns, and we're at the junction where I make a 90-degree, right-hand turn. We're only a couple of miles from the Coleman Ranch.

Robert "Bob" and his sons have carved out a large hop-growing and drying operation along with a fair-sized dairy. He's listened six or eight times to my reasons for getting "tanked up." They had a 1,250-gallon bulk tank for milk but really needed a 2,000. He knew it, and I felt he trusted me and wanted to do business with us. On one occasion we spent an hour and a half discussing everything from the right way to raise kids to the Near East policy of the United States. On another occasion, in the peak of the hop harvest, Bob took me on a personally guided tour of the complete operation from vines on trailers, through the drying process, to the final baling, along with the dozens of procedures in between. Each step of the way, with fifty or sixty people busy at their assigned positions, we moved our way through the many buildings and around all the machines with their vast assortment of pulleys, gears, belts and chains, each with its own unique sights, smells and sounds. I was given a tour that couldn't have been improved upon even for a visiting dignitary.

Uncle and I pulled into the driveway of our last dairy. I stopped the car, leaned over to Uncle, and said, "I'm going to try to sell this guy a milk tank, Uncle. I'll be back in a few minutes."

"How big?" was Uncle's immediate response.

"2,000," I replied impatiently.

"That's not big enough," countered Uncle. "Sell him a three or four thousand gallon. You can't tell when he might need it, and he might as well get it now and be done with it."

I've learned from experience not to pursue such advice further and just said, "I'll see what I can do."

One time Uncle had asked a prospective tank customer how many cows he had, and when he was told about 175, Uncle proceeded to tell him in no uncertain terms that the outfit needed a 40,000 gallon tank. Since the biggest tank we sold was a 6,000, and since the fellow could have gotten by nicely with a 2,000, needless to say I didn't sell the guy on the 40,000 idea. Remembering that rueful moment, I heard "Good luck," Uncle's parting words, and headed out to see if I could locate Bob. Not only did I locate Bob, but everything went perfectly. Even though he didn't know I was coming, it was almost as if he'd been standing waiting with contract-signing pen in hand. I spent a few minutes with him, explaining the details of the tank, and then he said, "Write it up." Almost in a daze I walked back to the car to draw up the contract. When I told Uncle that Bob had bought a tank from me, he said, "Good for you, Jerry, good for you."

I finished the paperwork and Bob signed it. I made a sketch of the milk house for our installation crew and drove away from the last dairy where Uncle would witness me make an extremely satisfying sale. Two months later, I was near the Coleman Ranch again and stopped by to see Bob. I caught him leaving the farm in one of his large trucks. He stopped when he saw me and we chatted for a few minutes. I told him that the day he bought his new tank was Uncle's last ride with me. He didn't say anything for a couple of minutes, and then, catching my eyes with a sensitive stare, said, "He was fortunate to have had someone who cared for him so much." I drove off knowing that he was thinking what some folks had verbalized, "I wonder if there will be anyone willing to look after me if I should live so long?"

8

DON'T CONFUSE ME WITH THE FACTS, MY MIND IS MADE UP

We headed due East from the Coleman's to Woodburn and the interstate freeway. Since it was getting close to lunch time, I figured we'd grab a bite after I called the home office with the order. We rounded the corner, passing on the left the golf course with the gray sand "greens" and off on the right the Woodburn drag strip. We then passed a housing tract just inside the city limits sign and crossed over the freeway to the collection of service stations, restaurants and shops that surround the Woodburn interstate exit. I made my call and then asked Uncle if he was hungry.

"Why sure," he said. "How about some soup?" which was his usual request when out on the road.

Knowing we'd have to get out of the car for that, which even under normal circumstances wasn't that easy, I said, "How about a fish sandwich instead?"

"OK," he agreed, and I swung into the Golden Arches, circled around to the drive-in window and placed the order - coffee, French fries, and a Filet of Fish for Uncle, and a Quarter-Pounder with cheese and a Coke for me. After a few minutes, we got the food and I pulled around and stopped in a convenient parking spot and turned the motor off.

Uncle hated to eat on the run, but there were times when we had had to travel so far in a day that we had to make every minute count. On those days, we'd grab a burger on the fly, but Uncle often objected so vigorously that a couple of times, though very hungry, he refused to eat. On one of his occasions of abstinence, I finally got so exasperated I exploded, "Uncle, you're stubborner than a Missouri mule!" Uncle sat silently for a few seconds and then said in a steady, firm voice, "I know it, and I wish I wasn't, but I am, and there's nothin' I can do about it!"

Uncle's stubbornness came through in many interesting and unusual ways—like the time he threatened not to go along selling milk tanks anymore unless I paid him at least ten percent of the selling price. He furthermore claimed that I wouldn't be able to sell a one without him. I tolerated this type of insult, comforting myself with the fact that "He's just an old man who really doesn't know what he's talking about." However, it's been seven months since Uncle left me, and about three and a half months since my sales dropped off to the point that I decided to get out of the dairy business and try something else. My wife, on occasion, reminds me of Uncle's words and then says, "Sometimes I think Uncle must be looking down from heaven trumpeting, 'I told ya that you couldn't sell tanks without me, Jerry!'"

Another occasion of Uncle's stubbornness began innocuously. He merely asked Judi what time she wanted to wake up. Judi realized that Uncle was going to take it upon himself to be her alarm clock. She also knew that he always was ahead of schedule by a couple of hours. So, since she wanted to get up at 5 a.m., she told Uncle, "How about 7 o'clock?"

"Fine, O.K.," agreed Uncle. It was two o'clock the next morning when I heard, from two floors below, the first faint "Yudi!" I rolled over, hoping he'd give up and go back to bed. No such luck. The next few calls were a bit louder. Then he ascended our spiral staircase, bellowing, "Yudi, Yudi," each step of the way.

He's got to give up soon, I thought, but no – he kept coming, stopping only long enough on the second landing to catch his breath. Then he began beating on the metal stair railing with his cane at each step, combining his calls with a few other words and phrases that he definitely hadn't picked up in church. When this approach got no response, he charged all the way to the third floor – right over to our bed. He banged his cane on the footboard of our brass bed, yelling in disgust, "Yudi, I'll never be your bell ringer again!" Indignantly, he turned and tromped back down the stairs, two flights to his bed below.

Strange surroundings were never Uncle's cup of tea. On one of our numerous but dreaded overnight runs to Sunnyside, Washington, Uncle came through in his typical fashion. Really, as I think back, he did extremely well, especially considering almost everyone else his age at best was in an old folks' home (or worse, depending on your viewpoint, pushing up posies.) Anyway, on this trip Uncle slept fitfully in the queen-sized bed we shared. He couldn't find a completely comfortable position, and as if that weren't bad enough, his pouch had sprung a leak. Finally, at three in the morning, he decided it was time to get up. I suppose that in itself wouldn't have been too bad, but he wasn't satisfied to be alone in his wakefulness; several pokes of his cane had me up, too.

Another time, under similar circumstances, he awoke at about the same time and was totally disoriented. He kept asking whose fool, crazy idea it was to come out in the middle of nowhere, leaving home's good board and bed for this. It took nearly an hour to settle him down, during which time he'd raised his voice several times. I got concerned that I'd get thrown in the pokey for second-childhood abuse.

His stubbornness was not merely a trait of his last days, either. Once, not long before Uncle came to live with us for good, I dropped by to see how he was getting along. To my surprise, I found one of Uncle's second cousins, who faithfully stopped by several times a week to check up on Uncle, sitting on a stool crying, water lapping at her feet. The water wasn't her tears, though that fact didn't help the general situation. "I told him not to use his wash machine," she sobbed. "It's got a leak in it someplace. But do you think he listens to me?" Uncle listens all right, but then he'd turn around and do just exactly what he wanted. Come hell or, in this case, high water, it had to be his way.

Coming back from a three-day company business meeting, and having made arrangements that Uncle be looked after in his own home while I was away, I stopped by to collect him. His second cousin, Ruth, who'd been almost constantly at his side, was totally exhausted and relieved beyond words to see me. I pleasantly greeted Uncle and said, "Are you ready to go back out to Sherwood?"

"Sherwood?" cried Uncle. "Why would I want to go out there?"

I tried explaining that Ruth couldn't stay with him any longer and he needed someone close by to give him a hand once in a while. Uncle wouldn't budge. I tried every tactic within reason, including a few that weren't, like threats of a rest home, but all were to no avail. Finally, I had to physically lift him up, which he fought with almost superhuman strength, knocking me about like a rag doll. Eventually he wore himself out and I was able to get him out to the car. From that point on, he was as cooperative as could be, but maybe only because he had formulated in his mind a way to get even. Several times after that, he'd bring up to different visitors various versions of the time he had been kidnapped. I wryly suggested that someone 98 years old would have to think of a different label that "kidnapping" to describe the event. However, he had dwelled on and retold the kidnapping incident enough times that finally it became a very real offense embellished with creative "extras" to heighten excitement and distort the facts.

It surfaced again in the large Tyee parking lot, a motel-restaurant-convention complex in Tumwater, Washington. The Tyee is large by most Northwest standards, containing several hundred rooms, two restaurants and bars, many large conference rooms, and surrounded by beautiful grounds with a gorgeous pool and bath house. The Tyee is situated just a few miles south of Olympia, Washington, the state's capital, and has developed a large clientele among those whose skills and services are required by government agencies. The interior is plush and in very good taste. Its excellent food and central location to our dairy market area, plus its amenities, cause our company to use its facilities frequently.

On that fairly warm day in the Tyee parking lot, Uncle sat in the Volare, dozing off and on, waiting for me to get out of a luncheon meeting with Jim Donavan, Elenbaas' regional sales manager. He'd had his lunch, and there was water in his cup that rested in the holder attached to his door, and I'd come out to check on him every twenty or thirty minutes. However, he finally decided he'd waited as long as he could and started honking the horn. He'd give three blasts and then wait. Of course I couldn't hear, but he certainly got the attention of a couple of elderly women who came over to the car to find out what was the matter but couldn't understand Uncle's Scandinavian accent. Seeing no one around who could assist them, they went into the motel lobby and called the local police. The police, one on a motorcycle, the other in a car, responded quickly and began questioning Uncle. At first Uncle told them he'd been kidnapped. The officers persisted in their questioning, asking Uncle who owned the car. He spoke what to them was an unintelligible flurry of syllables. Finally, they asked him if he could spell it.

"It's an old Youman name, and I'm not sure I can."

They went through his pockets, finding his wallet with his name and mine. They then went to the motel front desk and had me paged. When I arrived at the desk, the first thing I saw was the uniformed officers. "Oh no!" I thought and then said, "It's about my Uncle out in the car, isn't it?" Without waiting for their answer, I dashed out only to find Uncle serenely sitting in his usual place without a care in the world. The officers had followed me out, so I explained the circumstances, concluding by saying, "It's either a nursing home or he travels with me, and though this has its problems, I'd say this is a heck of a lot better." With compassion and apologies for any alarm they caused, they wished me well and drove their cycle and car away. A few minutes later, I, too, drove away with Uncle endlessly prattling, "What did those policemen say to you? What did they threaten to do?" for the three hours it took to get home.

Getting old is no fun. I know that as well as anybody could without being there yet myself. Uncle realized he needed some help. It made no difference that he'd been getting the help for some time already. He'd finally made the decision himself and appointed me to be in charge of him. "Jerry," he said. "You're to be in charge of me. Now sometimes I won't want to do what you say, so you'll just have to make me do it." I've heard understatements in my life, but this one wins the prize. We've all heard, "You can take a horse to water, but you can't make him drink." Well, in retrospect, I'd rather face a thousand dehydrated but thirstless horses than one obstinate old Ono.

At least Uncle made me famous, if only in our little community and with many of my customers. We were written up a couple of times in newspaper articles and on another occasion in our company's four page newsletter. The newsletter article included a reprint from one of the newspapers with a very nice picture of the two of us standing beside our trusty '78 Volare. Pleased, I made the mistake of showing the article and its picture to Uncle. He glanced at it, saw his picture, and blew up.

"Who gave permission to use my picture? I sure didn't! I was never asked. I never got anything for it. Boy, oh boy! I'm going to get my lawyer!" And he meant it.

Desperately, I talked and talked, finally concluding, "They didn't ask me, either."

"That's different," he logically said. "As a result of this article you'll get more business and make more money!"

What could I say? Finally, after several hours of bantering back and forth, he just clammed up, refusing to talk further. Fortunately, he eventually forgot about it.

My buying tickets to the Johnny Cash show evoked a similar response. One of my good friends had been going through a serious depression. I knew he was a Johnny Cash fan; in fact, he'd even named his only son Johnny, after Mr. Cash. When I heard that tickets were on sale a couple of months before a Portland concert, I bought enough for Mick and Patty, his wife, and Judi and myself. A couple weeks later, Mick was rushed into the hospital where they opened his skull and found an inoperable, malignant brain tumor. There was nothing they could do surgically, so they closed him up.

I was with his wife, Patty, and his three sisters and mother when the young surgeon came out into the hallway waiting area, eyes brimming, to give the family the bad news and very little hope to cling to. Patty just stood there like a recently-lost child, visible shaken but not yet sure of the extent or ramifications of her circumstances. Mick's mother turned white, began to wobble, and was assisted by one of the sisters to a nearby hard-backed chair, where she collapsed, cradling her face in her hands. The three sisters burst into tears, at first giving to and receiving support from one another; and then, as if to prove the textbooks right on the grieving process, their grief expressed itself in anger and they lashed out at one another. Finally, the doctors said they'd give him a couple weeks to recover from surgery and then schedule some radiation therapy.

I took Uncle in to visit Mick, since he'd come to know him quite well. In fact, he loved Mick very much, an affection Mick returned. They had gotten to know one another through church; also, every once in a while, Mick would spend the day riding out with us to visit dairymen. Of course, Uncle wanted to know all the details of Mick's hospitalization. When he heard about the cancer, he gasped and said, "Oh no, oh no, the poor ting, the poor ting." So before we visited Mick, I was very careful to remind Uncle that we surely didn't want to upset Mick by calling undue attention to his unfortunate condition. Uncle said rather indignantly, "I wouldn't do anything like that!" So I found him a wheel chair, trundled him up to the seventh floor of the hospital, and rolled him into Mick's room. Mick was sitting up at a forty-five-degree angle in his adjustable hospital bed. The top of his head was completely bandaged. I pushed Uncle in front of me, close to Mick's bedside. Pancake cap in place, cane between his legs, Uncle hunched slightly forward, squinting through his round wire-rim glasses, surveyed the bed and surroundings, and finally focused in on Mick. After we three exchanged a few uneasy greetings, Uncle leaned closer to the bed and confided, "Well, Mick, it won't be long until I'll be going up there, too." Mick just sat there with an uneasy half-smile on his face. Uncle leaned back, bowed his head, and as if thinking about the splendors of his future home, reverently closed his eyes. Unable to make myself disappear, I ignored the remark, changed the subject, and as tactfully as possible, hustled us out of there.

Anyway, I still had the tickets I'd purchased before anyone knew Mick had a cancerous tumor. I wasn't sure Mick would feel up to going, even to a concert featuring, as he called him, "My man in black, Johnny Cash." But I checked with his wife, she talked with the

43

doctors, and they thought the excursion was a great idea, giving Mick something to look forward to. Without telling anybody, I decided to take the "therapy" one step further; I composed a letter to Mr. Cash. I told him that, though I wasn't what he could call a fan of his, I had a good friend who had even named his son after him. I told him that this friend would be at his Portland, Oregon, concert after having just found out about an inoperable, malignant brain tumor and thus a very uncertain future. After dumping this load onto the printed page, I asked Mr. Cash if he could, even if so very briefly, meet my friend, Mick. After a few other, I hoped, appropriate remarks, I thanked Johnny regardless of the outcome of my request and prayerfully sent the letter off to the Grand Ole Opera, Nashville, Tennessee, by registered mail.

Meanwhile, I went about my regular activities, traveling around the Northwest, calling on dairymen, carrying the Johnny Cash tickets safely, or so I thought, in my wallet. For some reason that now escapes me, I took my wallet out to get something and then replaced it in my pocket. Somehow in that short time, those tickets slipped out. I didn't realize it until I saw Uncle intently studying something red and rectangular. As I continued driving along, I leaned over for a closer look.

"Hey, Uncle, those are mine," I said rather matter of factly.

"Yours?" said Uncle. "What do you mean? These Cash tickets are mine, not yours. Besides where would you get the dollars to buy these tickets? Don't you try to cheat me out of my money tickets!"

I begged and pleaded, laughed and cried, trying to explain who "Cash" was. But Uncle adamantly refused to hand them over and threatened me some more. Finally, after what had been up to that point continual rejection, out of the blue, Uncle just handed the tickets over.

A few days later, we received a telephone call from Johnny Cash's personal secretary who said they'd received my letter and were sending one to me. We received the letter the day of the concert. In it were instructions to ask for Johnny's stage manager by name, and he would see that Mick met Mr. Cash. As it turned out, all four of us met the Man in Black during a private audience just before he went out on stage. I can still see Mick's face as he visited with a person who'd given him hundreds of hours of listening pleasure and whom he now had met face to face. I snapped a picture of the two of them - Johnny with his black wavy hair, Mick with the long off-black nap of a fake fur hat covering his radiation-balded head.

My memories of Uncle are well-populated by instances of his intractability. Somehow, one morning, we got started off on the wrong foot. We had headed out early, before sunup, on our way to Hood River to see a customer who was having some milk tank problems. Uncle had refused to eat or drink anything before we left, so I laid in a good supply of toast and coffee and put a couple of bananas on the seat beside him. I figured if I didn't say anything, pretty soon he'd get over his snit, eat, and all would be fine. But we arrived in Hood River about an hour and a half from home, and Uncle still hadn't eaten. I stopped to place a phone call at a phone booth near the Hood River Inn right across the road from a Chevron station before we headed out to the dairy. Busy talking, I glanced towards the car. Uncle was gone! I abruptly ended the conversation, and as I hung up, I spotted Uncle walking in the middle of the street on the opposite side of the car. I frantically dashed out into the street to rush Uncle out of danger and get him back into the car, but he wouldn't budge. He jerked his arm away from me, made several threats, and shook his cane in my face. He refused to go anywhere near the car. Finally I grabbed him from behind and literally dragged him back to the car, Uncle twisting and threatening all the way. An older man (by any standard other than Uncle) stood less than twenty feet away, watching the whole episode, shaking his head. I'm sure he was thinking, "My, oh my, isn't it awful the way young people treat the older generation nowadays?"

I got Uncle into the car after several minutes of struggling. But once in, he'd open the door again and start to get out. Finally, snatching up a nylon tie which our installation crews used for securing piping, I rolled down both windows slightly on his side of the car, pushed the tie through both windows and around the middle post, and secured it so there was no way the door could be opened. Off we went, with Uncle still straining to get out the door. On the fifteen-minute trip to the dairy, I verbally launched into Uncle, telling him I couldn't understand his attitude. "Here I am," I cried, "doing the very best I can, keeping you from being put into a nursing home, and you're giving me all this trouble. What's wrong?"

Though I was experiencing the ugliest day of our entire relationship, my hardened heart began to soften as Uncle and I pulled onto the Don Carson dairy. The sun was brightly shining and the back forty on this well-cared-for dairy appeared to stretch out and melt into the northern slope of majestic Mt. Hood. The clear, crisp blue skies, the absolute whiteness of snow-highlighted by vein-like ridges that the wind had swept bare and black – and a few wispy clouds contrasted vividly to every imaginable shade of green. For the moment the morning's "Uncle Ordeal" appeared insignificant.

I shut the motor off and walked into the milk house. Don and his son-in-law welcomed me while donning knee-high rubber boots and yellow plastic, full-length aprons and jaunty baseball caps given each of them by the last tractor dealer who'd stopped by. We chatted briefly before getting down to the business at hand; and I was able, at the same time, to keep an eye on Uncle through a large window on the far end of the milk house. Don noticed my occasional glance and asked how Uncle was doing. I briefly explained the morning's events and together we watched as Uncle took his final pokes in his futile attempt to escape from the car. The Carson's had taken care of a retarded adult and, though their problems had been different from mine, they were extremely understanding about my situation.

Just before I finished up by solving the dairyman's tank problem, I noticed that Uncle had given up and was quietly eating his toast and drinking what by now had to be cold coffee. I vowed to myself that the point had finally come where I could no longer take care of Uncle. Other arrangements would have to be made. However, by the end of the day, which passed without further incident, Uncle's disposition was more than satisfactory and never reached those depths again. I'm glad to be able to say that I, like Uncle, could forget, too.

I never wore a safety belt as Uncle and I traversed the great Pacific Northwest. I'd figured Uncle was indestructible, much too stubborn to die in any mechanical contraption. After all, anybody who lived as long as Uncle wasn't about to check out in anything as unglamorous as an automobile crash. I joked that if perchance we had an accident, Uncle would be found, cap on head, cane in hand, poking around in the twisted rubble for my probably unrecognizable remains, muttering, "All right, Jerry, I know you're in there. Quit hiding! Get over here and give me your elbow so I can get back up to the highway." It never happened, of course, but Uncle did fall many times, only to bounce up again with no more than a slight bruise to show for his slip. When he did fall, it happened usually because of his insatiable curiosity which got him into situations where he didn't belong.

Sometimes, though, Uncle exercised a certain crusty caution. "Why don't you just give up? There's just too much snow on the ground. You'll never make it!"

I sometimes heard these encouraging words from Uncle. For example, I ventured out in a snowstorm trying to sell power take-off generators to dairymen struggling with flickering lights. Spinning, slipping and sliding, bouncing around in icy tracks made by earlier travelers, we somehow made it without so much as a minor incident. When we arrived safely back, I smugly pointed out, "Well, we're home, Uncle, and we didn't even have a fender bender."

"You were just lucky," sniffed Uncle. But luck wasn't the answer at all. Uncle had the most experienced guardian angel who had ever earned wings, an angel who could never sleep on the job.

Once, as I discussed with Uncle his unbending stubbornness, he said with a certain satisfaction, "You're not the only one who thought so. Some of the river pilots used to call me 'that curly-headed, Norsky son of a bitch.' I'd tell them to do it my way or get off the river!"

48

For real or imagined reasons, Uncle often got mad at me. My only salvation was that he spent so much time with me in so many different activities - selling trips on the road, living in our home, attending church with us, going out for pizza and beer, even taking in an occasional movie, being bathed and dressed by me – that Uncle often thought I was three or four different people. The advantage of his confusion was that when Uncle got mad, all I'd have to do is leave for a few minutes, come back to him and he'd spill his guts as to how "Jarry did this," "Gerri did that," or "Jerry did the other thing," and I could innocently sympathize with his mistreatment.

Before the pouch days, Uncle found holding his urine for any length of time presented a real problem – Uncle could be expected to cut loose almost any place. To make matters worse, he was by no means bashful about any part of his anatomy. His philosophy was, "If they've never seen it before, they won't know what it is; and if they have, seeing one more won't make any difference. So what the heck!" Once I parked on Main Street of Scio, Oregon, went to use a pay phone, and casually glanced back at the car. My horrified eyes saw Uncle, standing on the boardwalk-like sidewalk, relieving himself before any who dared look his way. I pretended I didn't notice and waited until he'd finished, climbed back in the car beside him, and beat it out of town, the noonday sun glinting reproachfully off Uncle's own Golden Pond.

On another occasion, I stopped to collect a several-month-old delinquent account, finding the only person home to be the dairyman's wife. But I soon noticed she wasn't paying much attention to me. Instead, she kept glancing over my shoulder towards the car. At first, I paid no heed, thinking this was her way of handling the unpleasant business of the overdue bill. When she promised a prompt payment, (the same promise I'd been given for months), I turned to return to the car and saw what had so distracted the debtor – the steam still rose from the puddle beside Uncle's side of the car, which faced the house. For Uncle, at least, the pressure of the moment had been relieved.

As it relates to his bouts of stubbornness, I'll also mention Uncle's total lack of patience with people or objects that got in his way. On our trips, he complained if it even looked as if someone were impeding our progress. "Get out of the way! What's wrong with you? Are you crazy? We want through!" And though he normally was a very gentle man, he once remarked, "I sure would like to show that guy a thing or two. If I had the chance, I'd club him in the head so hard that he'd never get up." Needless to say, on days like that, I'd be extremely careful not to cross him.

Despite his impatience and stubbornness, Uncle could also yield at least semi-graciously when necessary. You remember Mick, my friend with the brain tumor who'd met Johnny Cash. Well, not knowing what kind of shape he'd soon be in, we decided to take our wives on a long-planned trip to Hawaii. We made arrangements for Uncle to be looked after, but then came the problem. Uncle heard where we were going and wanted to come along.

"How much would it cost for me to come, too?" he asked.

"Too much." I said, groping for just the right combination of words to take the thought out of the realm of his further consideration. "It would take seven to eight hundred dollars, the flight would be long and tiring, and once we got there, we'll be jumping from place to place.

You wouldn't like it."

In spite of these obstacles, he persisted, unwilling to accept such flimsy excuses. "Oh, please! May I go?" he pleaded.

It took all the courage I could muster to overcome my guilt and Uncle's pleas before I finally prevailed. Uncle sighed and resigned himself to the fact that he wasn't going and then, which made Judi and me feel even worse, said, "Take a look at the coral reef in the harbor and let me know how much it's grown. I haven't been there since 1901 and it sure must have grown a lot since then."

We went, he stayed, we had a wonderful time, but we also made sure to bring back a picture postcard of the harbor on Oahu. It was still open after over 80 years of coral growth, and that was what Uncle was concerned about.

That wasn't our only trip without Uncle. I was being sent to Madison, Wisconsin, for a sales training school and managed to work it out so Judi could go along. We made arrangements to admit Uncle to the King City Care Center for the one week we were to be gone. I brought him over there Friday afternoon at 1:30 p.m. after a hurried sales trip to Tillamook early that same morning. We'd had to rush to get back in time to allow for all the necessary paperwork while there were still the staff members on hand to process them. It took quite a while to admit him, but after forty-five minutes I'd finally filled out the last line and signed the final form. By the time I'd finished, Uncle had been neatly deposited into his room. I went down, said goodbye, and left with the strangest feeling almost as if I were leaving part of myself behind. I checked back later that evening in an attempt to alleviate some of the guilt I was feeling. He was in his room, looking fine, and appeared pretty much as I had left him. I felt much better. The next day, before catching our plane, I stopped by again. I shouldn't have. I hardly recognized Uncle. I was told he had spent the whole night calling "Jerry", keeping his roommate awake most of the night. As if that weren't enough the staff couldn't be bothered with his "pecker" pouch, so they had him diapered and had wrapped him up in a dressing gown. He hadn't shaved, didn't know me or where he was, looked awful, and I began to wonder what I was doing to the man by leaving him. The staff assured me all would be fine once he adjusted, and since I'd postponed this training trip twice already, I decided I must go, hoping that somehow things would work out for Uncle.

Exactly one week later we got back and rushed to reclaim Uncle. At first we couldn't find him. After several dead-end hallways, I finally asked an attendant who directed me to the TV room. Although he didn't recognize me at first, when I finally got through to him he was more than ready to go home. I took him back to his room, got him dressed (pouch and all), and then whisked him out to the car. As we drove home, I asked Uncle how he liked the Care Center.

"I didn't!" he quipped. "They all just stood around asking me questions and laughing at me. I didn't like it one bit!"

However, when I made inquiries of the staff as to how Uncle did, they said that everyone had loved him. They appreciated his accent, his candid comments, his independent spirit, crazy moods, and the little flat cap that seldom left his head. It took several weeks of "recovery", but finally Uncle got over his seven-day "exile". He didn't have to go back again until the last few days of his life when, as it turned out, he wasn't able to recognize anybody, let alone be bothered by where he was staying.

9

A LOAF OF BREAD, A JUG OF WINE
. . . AND UNCLE

Uncle loved to eat. Even this last trip, in spite of his acute physical problem, this day was no exception. He slurped his coffee and wolfed down his French fries, complaining only mildly that the almost-white potatoes were a bit under-salted. I finished first and then waited, listening to the radio, thinking of all the mounds of food Uncle had gone through in his lifetime.

Uncle would actually eat most anything. In spite of that fact, there were times that Uncle's taste buds, for whatever reason, would reject good food, while other times he'd relish the same item, claiming it couldn't be better. One such occasion was the time my extremely generous good friend Roy Loughary, owner of A-1 Electric in Portland, gave us coupons for a hamburger and Coke at the fast-food chain across the street from his store. Uncle took two or three bites of his burger and then expressed his appreciation by saying, "If there was a dog around here, I'd feed the rest of this sandwich to 'em. The meat's so coarse they must be using horse meat." I think Roy, who had a fantastic sense of humor, enjoyed hearing about that remark more than the hundreds of sincere "thank yous" that he'd received from his large group of loyal customers.

Uncle was hard to please on another occasion, too - A company dinner at the Hadley House in Tillamook, with several of our business clients and personnel from the dairy supply company. Uncle responded loudly to a question about how he liked the food with "Not very well. I've never tasted tougher pork chops." In fact, the unfortunate Hadley House didn't seem to please him at all. We stopped there for lunch a few months later, and Uncle requested that he be brought a sandwich while he'd stay in the car. I sat near a window so I could keep an eye on him, and when the waitress brought the meals, I ran Uncle's lunch out to him. About a third of the way into our own lunches, I glanced out the window just in time to watch Uncle pitch his sandwich out of the car, one piece at a time, the fragments piling up conspicuously in the restaurant's parking lot.

In a similar incident at the Tyee in Olympia, Washington, Uncle decided to come in and eat. But after having taken a few bites, he complained to the waitress, "The food you brought me isn't fit to eat." I tried smiling and making light of the remark, but the woman glared at us with a look that said if we'd already left our departure still wasn't soon enough.

Fruit, however, was one of Uncle's favorite foods, so when we were near Chehalis, Washington, one hot summer day, Uncle had me stop at a stand and buy several pounds of Bing cherries. They were big and black, just bursting with juice and extremely flavorful. Uncle immediately started popping them in as fast as his hands could travel from sack to mouth. The seeds rat-tat-tatted as he spat them against the dash and they rained onto the floor. After about fifteen minutes, with no reprieve in sight, I finally suggested that he stop before he developed a fatal case of the runs. Unbelievably, without so much as a word of objection, he stopped eating, closed up the bag, and placed it on the seat between us. About that time I'd reached another dairy, so I stopped and went in, leaving Uncle to wait in the car. When I came out and looked towards the car, Uncle was nowhere to be seen.

"Oh, no!" I said to myself. The driveway to the dairy had been cut into a hill and there was a steep bank on Uncle's side of the car. It sloped forty feet down into a rocky gully. Would I find Uncle lying in a broken, bloody heap among the brush and boulders below? I rushed out to the Volare and breathed a sigh of relief and a chuckle at the same time. There was Uncle lying across the seat, out of sight of anyone except the most careful observer, popping cherries and spitting seeds with piston-like precision.

His single-mindedness about food manifested itself in other ways, too. Once Uncle got in his mind that he wanted to eat, he had no patience. If he arrived at the table and the meal wasn't all ready, he'd give a person about two and a half minutes to produce food. Then he'd push abruptly away from the table, chair screeching, exclaiming, "Too late, I don't want it now!"

"But, Uncle, it's coming!" I'd say in exasperation.

"So is Christmas!" Uncle would snort. "So is Christmas!" He'd push himself from the table and off he'd go.

Uncle's impatience ran rampant at home, too. We'd run out of bread, which wasn't too uncommon since Uncle could go through as much as a loaf a day. Judi had fixed some clam chowder and gave it to him with the last three crackers she'd been able to find. Uncle took one look at her offering and said, "Where's the bread?" Hearing that we were out, Uncle mumbled that we were just throwing an old man soup and crackers out of penury, and then reached for his wallet. Thinking he had forty dollars and finding only two, his anger turned to ugliness.

"You've been stealing from me!" He shouted. "I had forty dollars in my purse, and now it's gone."

I carefully explained how he'd spent part of the twenty, not forty, on meals that week while we had been on the road. I also told him that out of the goodness of his heart, without any outside encouragement, he'd given the girls a five dollar bill each. Now all he had left was two dollars, but in a couple of days he'd be getting another twenty in the mail. I wasn't able to convince him completely, but with only a few additional accusations and threats, he turned his attention to the real problem at hand – No bread. He gave Judi his last two dollars and insisted she or someone else immediately jump in the car, rush to the store, and buy some more bread.

As I said, it wasn't uncommon for us to run low on or out of bread. We did this many times. I usually could fill in with that one last hot dog bun jammed in the back of the freezer, or the neglected heel or two wadded up in an otherwise-empty plastic bag. This time, several weeks after the previous incident, all I could find were two rather desiccated slices left in a bread bag that had been hidden behind some things in the cupboard. Try as I might with moisture and microwave, I couldn't' revitalize those former staffs of life. I explained this situation to Uncle, and he seemed understanding as he sat down to what otherwise was a perfectly acceptable meal. I should have saved my breath. He got through half of one slice, dropping the remainder with a clunk onto his clean plate. He picked up the other, broke it loudly in half, stuck it in his pocket and said, "I'm going to take this with me to my coffin and show the Lord just exactly how you've been treating an old man down here."

Coffee had no close competition in Uncle's opinion. He'd say that the brew made from that bean was "God's greatest gift to man." But even coffee led to embarrassing moments for me. On one occasion we were in a restaurant in Gaston, Oregon, enjoying soup, a sandwich, and of course coffee. The coffee had been served in tea-cup-style, off-white porcelain ware, a bad choice as far as Uncle was concerned. He flagged down the waitress and said, "These cups are for children, not grown men! What's wrong with you people?" The teenaged girl looked him over and then turned and quietly said to me, "Is he for real?"

Once a month, I'd meet with my boss over breakfast in the Oregon coastal town of Tillamook. Sometimes Uncle would join us; other times, because he already had eaten or preferred having something brought to him, he'd stay in the car. This particular time he decided to come in. Once inside, he exchanged only minimal pleasantries with my boss and then got down to the serious business at hand, namely eating. Fortunately for all concerned, the waitress took our order quickly, and while he was waiting for his scrambled eggs and pancakes, he gulped down several cups of his favorite – coffee. I'd laced it with milk to cool it off so he could drink it faster. Finally, his breakfast came and he dove in with enthusiasm. With an occasional nudge by me, his almost-blindly-guided fork came up with something on it each trip and Uncle worked his way steadily through his meal.

After finishing the food and washing it down with a couple more cups of coffee, he started impatiently tapping his cane. About five minutes passed, but we still had some business yet to discuss. Uncle, however, had had it. He struggled up, refusing help, saying he was going to the car, " . . . and if it was me that owned this place, I'd tell you fellas to get the hell out of here!" With that, he tromped out to the car.

Sometimes, though seldom really sick, Uncle would become nauseated. On one such occasion we were having lunch at the Kelso Thunderbird, one of our nicest chains of restaurants and inns on the West Coast. Half way through the meal, Uncle said, "I think I'm going to puke." Sure enough, I was just barely able to jump up and get around to his side of the table when he started to spout. I grabbed his napkin and was able to catch some of it and direct the major portion onto his plate. I carefully cleaned Uncle up with my napkin and then covered the whole mess with a dry napkin, making it look like Uncle had finished. I then got him up and hustled him through the tables, around the corner, and down the hall to the restrooms. I stood with him over a toilet, just in case his stomach had more to reject. When all appeared O.K., I sat him down in one of the stalls, telling him to stay there while I went back in to settle our account. When I got back to our table, the waitress had neatly and efficiently cleaned up Uncle's side, leaving my half-finished lunch with a new napkin and fresh coffee. I gratefully but hastily finished, paid the bill, and then dug down extra deep for a generous tip for a kind young lady who went well above and beyond the call of duty. Within minutes I had collected Uncle and we were on the road again, not too much worse for the wear.

One time, before Uncle came to stay with us for good, he

suddenly decided he wanted me to take him home. Judi, feeling a bit hurt and wanting to find out why he wanted to leave, asked, "What's wrong, Uncle? Is there anything I can do?"

"No," replied Uncle. Then, "Lots of things." He went on, "The food around here, for example, is not very good." As if that wasn't bad enough, he capped it off by saying, "It will be a cold day in hell before I ever come back!"

Though we tried, when Uncle made up his mind, we might as well save our energy. So we helped him get all packed up, and I drove him home to Portland. I helped him up the steps of his home on aptly, ironically-named Failing Street, unlocked the door, and assisted him into his living room. Then I stepped back and watched, suddenly realizing the reason for his earlier disgust and discontent. Uncle had been homesick. Soon he scurried around as fast as his four-score-and-sixteen-year-old legs would carry him. He was as happy as an old hen in her nest. At that time, he still was pretty well able to care for himself, so after checking that he had plenty of everything, which his second cousin Ruth had taken care of, I bid him farewell, reminding him he was always welcome out in Sherwood.

A few days later, I got the very last letter Uncle was ever to write to me. The name and address were so shakily written that I was amazed it got to us. It said, "Portland, Oregon. May 19, 1978. Dear Judy and Gary, I am ready to go up again anytime. When you are ready to come down after me. Please let me know. My phone is 292-6278, Portland, Oregon." He hadn't even remembered to sign it. The next day, after calling, I went to pick him up at our mutually-agreed time. I walked up the steps and peered into the front window. There sat

Uncle. He was fully dressed, including jacket and overcoat. His cap lay on the chair closest to the door. With his suitcase at his feet and folded hands resting on the cane that stuck between his legs, he was awaiting my arrival. He greeted me with a hug and big smile and an exuberance that even exceeded the happiness I'd witnessed a few days earlier. I couldn't wait to share with Judi the warmth, enthusiasm, and anticipation Uncle now had for coming back out to his new home in Sherwood.

Uncle would eat almost anything, but when he knew someone else was picking up the tab, he could turn into a real gourmet. Several times when he had been taken out for a nice but what was not to be an extravagant meal, he'd got a bit carried away. Aunt Dee and Uncle Al, down for a day or two from Tacoma, were often his victims. They ended up more than once suggesting that he order something other than the couple of lobster tails that Uncle had decided on. Uncle's all-time favorite, however, was basic and very contemporary – pizza and lots of beer, with an occasional taco, providing I put enough hot sauce on it. He'd complain if it wasn't super-spicy, voicing his complaint loudly enough so all could hear that the taco just didn't have enough "kick".

The last few months of his life still included pizza, but he had trouble remembering what it was called. He'd say, "Jerry, let's go out and get some of that flat, triangular stuff."

"Do you mean pizza, Uncle?"

"Yeah, that's the stuff-peasa pie."

On the way back home from a few days' visit with my dad, who doesn't allow beer to be consumed in his house, Uncle insisted that we stop at one of the first watering holes we came to. He sat there with a neat ring of foam bubbles decorating his recently-moistened lips and said, "Boy, oh boy, Ted doesn't know what he's missing. I'll bet if he tasted one, he'd love it."

Uncle also loved seafood, especially oysters and crab. I know he'd have some company in his method of eating raw oysters, but the way he'd eat crab was another story. I don't mean to imply that Uncle ate raw crab. He was very careful that it was well-cooked, but that's where conventional crab-eating, at least for everyone else I've watched, stopped. Before the crab cooled off, he'd dive in and devour everything but the gills and shells. He'd use the main oval body shell as a bowl, and then carefully catch all the green slime as he broke apart the crab and savored every last drop and morsel of meat. He sucked out every speck and fiber before throwing anything into his growing pile of scraps. I guess it's good that he enjoyed it so much, because once he got started, his appetite had to make up for all the others whose enjoyment was postponed until Uncle was finished and their stomachs settled.

While Uncle was at his own home, he ate big and, generally speaking, quite well; that was in spite of the fact that at times the vegetables were wilted, the fruit mushy, the lunch meat a bit over-aged and the cheese had a speck or two of uncalled for mold. His most frequent from-scratch recipe was his stew. He'd fill a large kettle half full of water and then start adding such ingredients as quartered but unpeeled potatoes, several unscrubbed carrots cut three to four inches long, rutabagas cut in half, three or four onions with only part of the outer wrapper removed, lots of salt and pepper, and a few stray chunks of meat. He would start simmering it early in the day, and by late afternoon or early evening it was ready. Judi and the girls wouldn't touch the finished product, but I, like Uncle, have a cast-iron stomach, so we'd both dive in, using a slice or two of stiff bread Uncle had gotten the week before to help soak up all the juice.

It's fitting that I'm now closing out my "Uncle and food" stories with the account of our one and only breakfast stop at the same fast-food chain at which we are eating our last lunch together. For an inexpensive and quick breakfast I had stopped at a McDonald's. After getting Uncle inside and seated, I ran my eyes through the menu, trying to read it all from where I had found our seats. I should have gotten up and left when Uncle kept asking when the girl was coming to take our order. I <u>really</u> should have left when he repeated rather rudely, "You mean this is self-service?" He finally settled down and opted for the sausage and pancakes with, of course, coffee. I thought that my speedy delivery of his breakfast would more than make up for the lack of full service. Wrong again. The pancakes were too tough, the sausage didn't have enough zing and, "If I go to a restaurant, I expect to be waited on. I don't like this serve yourself business one little bit!"

10

SECRET OF UNCLE'S LONGEVITY: IT'S
NOT IMPORTANT WHAT YOU DO, JUST DO IT
FOR A LONG TIME!

U ncle's finished now with his lunch, so I start the car and weave
through the parked cars and into the street. We turn left on the
road that, if we had gone the other way, would have taken us past
Woodburn High School to 99 East and the main part of Woodburn.
We precede only a hundred feet or so and turn right, picking up the I-5
freeway heading north. The next stop is the medical offices at
Meridian Park Hospital where Dr. Morita has his office. The time had
really flown by. It was 1:45; we'd have to hurry to make it on time.

Down through the course of his century, Uncle had many and
varied encounters with medicine men and, most recently, medicine
women. He talked with me at great length about numerous visits to
doctors and, in several cases, the hospital.

He told me of the time in Fort Blakley that he almost earned an
early grave. He was working for a lumber mill whose dock jutted out
some distance into the water. His was a night shift, and Uncle went
out on the dock to get something he needed inside. It was very dark
and, unknown to Uncle, someone had removed several boards of the
decking. Before he knew what was happening, he plunged down into

the water and debris that was awash under the dock. Bruised, sore, and very cold, clinging to a scrap of timber, Uncle bobbed in the water under the pier. Finally, after what seemed like hours, someone hard his cries and came running.

"How did you get down there?" was the would-be rescuer's response.

"I fell," said Uncle. "How did you think I got down here, jump? Get me out of here!"

"How can I do that?" inquired the man.

"Get a rope!" yelled Uncle.

"Where is one?" replied the guy.

Between chattering teeth, Uncle carefully explained where the fellow could find one, and eventually he was dragged to safety. Uncle said he felt so cold that he wondered if he could ever get warm again. The doctor found no broken bones but lots of abrasions and bruises, and fearing that Uncle would suffer from shock and contract pneumonia, he sent Uncle to his cabin and bed. Several weeks passed before he finally recovered sufficiently to continue his duties at the mill.

On another occasion, while working on a road crew in Seattle, Uncle was a little too close to the cement mixer when a part gave way and the hopper came down, just missing his head but not his left foot. One third of that foot had been crushed and Uncle was whisked off to the hospital. The doctors did what they could for the foot, but each day it looked worse. Finally, they came to Uncle and said that they had decided to amputate his foot just above the ankle.

"Oh, no, you don't!" Uncle said. "That's my foot, and I'll be the one who decides what's to be done with it! And I'll tell you this, it will not be amputated! I'll die first!"

After a lengthy exchange, these doctors finally gave up, refusing to have anything more to do with such an uncooperative patient. Uncle, not to be denied, located a physician who agreed, after extensive re-examination and Uncle's continual insistence, that a further attempt be made to save his foot. "Listen," said the new doctor, "you'll have to work with me, follow my orders, change your attitude, or we won't get anywhere." Uncle agreed and the doctor went to work. He cut off all the mangled meat and bones, which included his toes, preserving as much as possible of the skin on the top side of the foot. This he pulled over what was left and, along with a skin graft taken from Uncle's leg, secured everything to the underside of the foot.

"Oh, it stunk!" remembered Uncle. He was to spend an entire year in a Tacoma Catholic Hospital. One of the Sisters who cared for Uncle was totally smitten by him. She even went so far as to say that she'd give up her position as a nun if Uncle would become a Catholic and marry her. Uncle said, though she was very nice and took very good care of him and showered him with hugs and kisses, "I was born a Lutheran and I'm going to die a Lutheran." The doctor was true to his word and Uncle turned into a model patient. Just before Christmas, twelve months later, Uncle was discharged from the hospital, able to walk unassisted on a still very functional foot. He told me the first thing he did was go out and buy the biggest bouquet of red roses he could find and personally deliver them to the doctor, saying, "You've given me the best Christmas gift I've ever had."

"Dr. Lester" was Uncle's general practitioner prior to his

coming out to live with us. He had a rather unusual personality for an M.D., and I would say that's very fortunate for the medical profession. The fact that he was overweight, sloppy in appearance and hygiene, and had manners that left much room for improvement was superseded the day a horrified Judi showed me a newspaper clipping about him. His license was on the line due to a number of accusations leveled at him by his office nurse. She claimed that he continually propositioned her, often chasing her around the office. She also accused him of urinating in the office sinks, plus many other improprieties for a man in his position (or any position, as far as that goes).

On one occasion when Uncle still lived on his own, I got a call from him complaining that he didn't feel well. He asked if I'd come over and take him to the doctor. I knew immediately that something was desperately wrong. Uncle never complained about being sick, and never before or since had he asked to be taken to the doctor. So I rushed over from where we were living at that time, some forty minutes away, wondering what I'd find and especially concerned about getting there before he expired. I dashed up the steps into the house, let myself in, and found Uncle alive but not at all well. He complained of stomach cramps, and his skin color was a ghastly yellow-gray. I slipped his coat and hat on him, got him into the car, and drove as fast as legally possible to "Dr. Lester's" office some thirty to forty blocks away. Since I had phoned ahead, they were expecting us and in no time at all we were ensconced in an examination room. "Dr. Lester" began his examination by poking the largest finger on his right hand up Uncle's largest lower orifice. It didn't take two premed students to figure out that he wasn't checking for hemorrhoids. I anxiously awaited the diagnosis. Uncle's problem was that his prostate gland had completely closed off his bladder from the urinary tract, causing fluid waste to back up. "Dr. Lester" called Woodland Park Hospital and made arrangements for Uncle's admittance.

He told me to pick up a few of Uncle's personal items and then take him to the hospital. On the way to his house, I swung by Ruth and Esther's to let them know what was happening, but they weren't home. "They must be getting their hair done," I thought to myself. As it turned out, they had been at the hair dresser's, but had walked there, something unusual for them. Ruth had finished first and started on home. Then, at about the same time I was at "Dr. Lester's" with Uncle, Ruth was seeing a doctor. A block and a half from home she had been mugged, knocked to the ground with such force that her shoulder was dislocated, and her purse snatched. She lay writhing in pain for thirty minutes, watching people actually crossing over to the other side of the street to avoid any involvement. Finally, a Good Samaritan motorist equipped with a CB radio stopped and called an ambulance. Ruth spent two weeks in the hospital, took therapy for months, and even five years later continues to have pain.

Unaware of all this, I left, promising myself I'd call them later. I picked up Uncle's things and drove to the hospital. It had been about an hour since we'd left the doctor's office, and "Dr. Lester" had been waiting for us for over thirty minutes. A bit upset at our delay, he demanded, "What kept you so long?" Until then, I hadn't realized the severity of Uncle's condition. During the delay, his bladder could have burst!" "Lester" informed me that he had contacted a Dr. Saco, who turned out to be one of the finest practitioners in his particular field.

Nurses rushed Uncle off and left me to take care of the paperwork. When I finished, I was directed to Uncle's room, where to my relief I found him resting comfortable in bed. A catheter had been forced through the obstruction and was thus relieving the pressure. Dr. Saco met with me to explain that Uncle's prostate gland would have to be partially removed. Though the surgery wasn't uncommon or difficult, Uncle's age made even more routine surgery potentially fatal. Dr. Saco then went on to say, "Your Uncle's heart is awfully weak, so I'd like to give him a chance to build himself up a bit, here in the hospital, before performing the surgery." Three days later, after I had made several harried trips shuttling between the two different hospitals Ruth and Uncle were in, his operation was successfully performed.

Uncle later was to refer to this surgery quite often. He loved to tell to any who'd listen how " . . . they just numbed me with a shot and up the penis they went! Dr. Saco went snip, snip, and opened up the – what was that thing, Jerry, Dr. Saco cut on?"

"The prostate gland, Uncle," I'd reply.

"That's it! He opened up the prostate gland and I could urinate again. I was awake and watched the whole thing."

Uncle had remained in the hospital for over two weeks. During that stay, he endeared himself to many people, especially to one of his roommates and his family. I didn't learn of this affection until I took Uncle back for his post-surgery examination. During the visit, Dr. Saco took me aside and said, "Your Uncle did more for a millionaire patient of mine than I've ever been able to do." He went on to explain, "The patient of mine who shared Uncle's two-man room was an extremely wealthy pharmaceutical magnate who'd made his fortune in the Hawaiian Islands. Periodically, he had me admit him into the hospital, fearing his minimal aches and pains were something serious. He demanded and got the best of care, all of which your Uncle got a first-hand view. Finally, after several days, your Uncle said to him, "There's nothing wrong with you. The problem is you're only thinking about yourself all the time. You ought to think about others and you'd be much better off. See that book on your table there? That's a Bible. You should read it. It would do you a lot of good!"

As fate would have it, though I don't believe in fate, on that same day as we were leaving, we met the wealthy man's wife and daughter who were coming to keep an appointment. Adorned with silk, furs, and glittering rings, they hugged, squeezed, and kissed Uncle as if meeting a favorite relative after a long separation.

Though Uncle, especially compared to most people, got along fine without much assistance from doctors, he valued their skill. However, he took advantage of their services only when his own remedies failed. His years spanned a past day and age with a relatively small amount of specialized medicine to the present when we often seem to need a different doctor for each of our two nostrils. The contrast has always amazed me, but Uncle made these transitions without batting an eye. A blood clot developed in his leg once, and finally the pain and swelling got so bad that he agreed to go to his doctor. "Dr. Lester" took one look and, knowing he'd have trouble getting Uncle to take the treatment said, "If we don't do something quick, I'll have to amputate your leg."

True to form, bringing back memories of his mutilated foot, Uncle snapped back, "Nobody is going to touch that leg, and if anyone would, it sure wouldn't be you. You're just a pill doctor, not a surgeon. Can't you give me some sort of medicine to dissolve the clot?"

Whether the doctor was paving the way for what he'd been planning to do all along or just threatening him with the most drastic of treatments so he'd be willing to take the least drastic, I can't say. But since Uncle had outlined the mode of treatment himself, he was willing to be admitted into the hospital without a whimper. In a matter of days, the problem was taken care of. However, though his recovery was complete, its side effects caused weakness, loss of memory, and general physical instability. Those symptoms confined Uncle to his bed for a number of days. Judi, Ruth, and Esther wondered if this inability to bounce back was an indication of his age. All three felt that Uncle perhaps had reached the proverbial "end of the line". But I believed that all the chemicals had upset his system's balance and once enough time had passed, the effects would disappear and he'd be fine. Nevertheless, they discussed rest homes and what type of funeral arrangements would need to be made. Sure enough, five years later, Uncle died.

Apart from these few medical emergencies, Uncle had very few contacts with doctors and hospitals. In fact, the only other time I can remember his talking about them, other than the incidents already mentioned, was the time in the late twenties when he was hit in the head by a hook attached to a cable. The blow occurred during his years on the dredge. He was supervising as first mate when he came upon a couple of fellows wrestling when they should have been watching the winch yarding in a piece of dredge piping. One of the fellows, Uncle recalled, was a Swede who prided himself in having soft hands. Uncle asked him how he got and kept them that way; upon hearing the guy's method, he was sorry he asked. The Swede said he urinated on them regularly. Anyway, before Uncle could do any more than just yell, "Stop fighting!" the pipe had come too far and got jammed, but the winch kept cranking. Finally, something snapped, causing the hook on the cable to rifle toward Uncle, grazing his head. An inch closer would have spelled out a death certificate. As it turned out, he lost the sight in his left eye and several weeks of work.

Before I leave this phase of Uncle's medical meandering, I'd better throw in a plug for a branch of the medical business that before Uncle I'd never heard about. This is the podiatrist or "foot doctor," as Uncle called him. I took Uncle a time or two and observed the whole procedure. The podiatrist clipped the nails on Uncle's only good foot and then used special clippers, knives, and scissors to slice away build-ups of calloused skin on the toed foot and on the underside of the one without toes.

When Uncle took up permanent residence with us, once or twice a week (depending on when I could talk him into it), I'd give him a shower and check his feet. His big toenail was one-half an inch thick and needed a special podiatrist's tool which I didn't have. I managed, however, with a big pair of clippers, by taking a little bit of nail at a time. The three middle toes were as gnarled as a hundred years of use would make almost anything. Even worse, however, was the little one. It skewed off at a forty-five degree angle from the direction it should have been and pointed towards the outside of the foot, not the middle, before it circled back. Try as I might, I never did make that nail appear to belong to anything human. The last thing I did was to clean out the cracks and crevices around and in between Uncle's toes. His toe-jam stunk worse than limburger cheese, and usually days passed before my hands smelled normal.

11

JUST FOR THE HEALTH OF IT

We're nearing Wilsonville now, and the traffic's beginning to pick up. It's a good thing we're not still using the old system for disposing of Uncle's fluid wastes or there would be a lot of yellow cars behind us. With Uncle's bladder problems, prior to Pouch Day, we'd use a urinal. When Uncle told me he had to "get rid of some water" while we still were driving down the road, I'd haul out the urinal from under the seat, Uncle would unzip, and whatever fluid he had left (that hadn't already leaked out, or been lost while taking aim, or spill while we bounced along) I threw out the window. You can imagine the sight. A window is rolled down, out jets a mist of yellow moisture rooster-tailing out behind the speeding brown Volare. If wind conditions weren't just right, a good deal of the fragrant mist would blow right back into the car.

Well, at least that's not going to happen today, and we're now passing the Burns Brothers Truck Stop next to Vip's across from a Holiday Inn on the opposite side of the freeway. We'll have to get into the right lane soon, but first we'll pass the 205 Freeway exit to Oregon City and Southeast Portland. We're past that exit, move into the far right lane, and take the Tualatin off-ramp. We stop at the light, look to the left, and take a free righthand turn. We're now heading east toward Meridian Park Hospital and the Annex where Dr. Morita's office is located. The hospital is just a couple of country blocks off the freeway and already visible on the hillside. When the hospital and its adjoining annex were first build, all you could see surrounding their buildings, were cows, crops, and an occasional rural home. Now as we head up the hill to the right are hundreds of condos and apartments and in behind them, several new housing developments. A few open patches still remain, including the floodplain's lowlands in behind the Buffalo Head Tavern and a leftover field or two where one may still catch a glimpse of a few head of livestock and a suburban horse or two. We finally turn left onto the hospital grounds, wind up the hill past the A-frame that's now being used, in part, by the hospital's women's auxiliary.

Judi had had to stop there once, not many weeks earlier, to take care of some business when Uncle and I had been along. Judi went on in while Uncle and I remained in the car. Finally, after fifteen minutes, I went in to see what the delay was. Judi assured me she'd be out shortly, so I went back out to the car. Uncle asked what the women did in there and I tried to explain. I'm sure I didn't do a very good job of explaining, but I did my best. In another fifteen minutes I went back in, again to see what the holdup was, about fed up with an Uncle who was beginning to lose his patience. Judi assured me that she wouldn't be much longer, so once again I went back out to the car and Uncle.

"What's keeping her?" Uncle asked.

I tried explaining, but since I didn't know much myself, the explanation didn't make much sense. Twenty minutes of grumbling, a lot of neck craning, and impatient rapping of his cane on the underside of the dash, Uncle finally reached his limit. He made a couple of quick gestures with his hands and said, "Let's get out of here! There's something going on in there, and I'm sure it's not legal!" A few minutes later, Judi finally came out. When I told her of Uncle's suspicions, she laughed and said she just couldn't wait to share his accusations with the Ladies of the Auxiliary. Later, she told me about the chuckles Uncle's comment brought to those women, whose most illegal activities are parking too long in front of their furrier as they prepared for their next society function.

We climbed the hill and made two more left turns before we're in the annex parking lot. I stopped right in front of Dr. Morita's office and went in to see if I could borrow a wheelchair. Dr. Morita's fair-haired, fair-skinned office nurse, Jeannine, dressed in her usual crisp, clean, white uniform, looked pleasantly at me through her large, contemporary, plastic framed glasses and said, "I'm sorry, Gary, but we don't have one, but the hospital's emergency department right next door does, and I'm sure they would let you borrow one."

I went back to the car and told Uncle where I was going and that I'd be right back. Emergency lent me the chair and quickly I wheeled it back to the car. I carefully helped Uncle into the chair and wheeled him into Dr. Morita's office. Two other people occupied the waiting room. One was a man older than I who held the door open for us. He also helped me find a spot to park Uncle's wheelchair and make sure that he was comfortable. His helpfulness reminded me that I could never have done what I'd been doing for Uncle without the help of others, including those whose names I never knew.

Jeannine then handed me the paper work, and I quickly filled out the few forms. Handing the sheets back reminded me of an incident of a couple months earlier when Dr. Morita's office had been contacted by the Woodburn Police. I was at "J's" restaurant collating the final details of an installation of a heat recovery system with the owner, Jim Goldt. I had left Uncle in the car for what had been intended as a short wait, but one thing led to another and before I knew it, forty-five minutes had flown by. When I realized how long I had tarried, I rushed out to check on Uncle, but I was too late to stop the chain reaction already in motion. Naturally, Uncle had tired of waiting. He had climbed out of the car, moved just enough so that he could slam shut the car door, and then, can in hand, pancake cap pulled down over his forehead, he leaned back against the car and tried to remember his name and where he was. About that time, a burly trucker walked by on his way in for a cup of coffee. He noticed Uncle and asked if he needed some help. Uncle's confused reply left no doubt that Uncle was in need of some assistance. As they talked, the group began to grow. By the time I got out there, a tow-truck driver, two policemen, and a couple of additional restaurant patrons had joined the trucker. They had found Uncle's identification bracelet that I'd left on him from the time he stayed in the Care Center while Judi and I were in Madison, Wisconsin. On that bracelet were not only Uncle's name but the Care Center's and Dr. Morita's. Well, as you've been able to guess by now, the police contacted by radio not only the Care Center, which really couldn't be of much help, but finally Dr. Morita himself. True to form as relaxed and composed as he always is, he told them that they had nothing to be alarmed about. They had merely encountered the famous "Uncle Charlie," and therefore, Gary Gorsuch was somewhere close and would be out to check on him soon. It so happened, just as they were wrapping up this conversation, I walked rather briskly onto the scene. Jeannine and I had a good laugh as I was able to give her the whole picture from the other end of the phone.

When it was our turn to go into an examination room, Jeannine held the door open. We turned left down the short hall. Dr. Morita's office is on the right; the nurses' desk with files and all their paraphernalia is on the left. We passed a door on the right and proceeded to the last door on the left. Jeannine pushed it open for us and I wheeled Uncle in. She then told us that Lloyd would be with us in a few minutes. I passed the time by talking with Uncle.

"You like Dr. Morita, don't you, Uncle?"

"Yes, he's a very fine doctor," agreed Uncle. "Those Yapaneese are very smart people."

"How are you feeling, Uncle?" I asked.

"Fine," answered Uncle. Then, raising his voice an octave or two, boasted, "I feel good all the time."

Dr. Morita walked in, giving the appearance that we were his only concern and that he had all the time in the world to take care of us. "Hello, Charles," he said, knowing that he needed to speak up and direct the sound close to Uncle's ear. "Have you been getting enough beer and pizza pie lately?"

"Oh, sure," said Uncle. He then cocked his head in Lloyd's direction and said, "Do you like that stuff, too?"

"Why, of course!" replied Dr. Morita. Then, "You're not feeling too well, Gary tells me."

"Oh, I don't know," said Uncle. "I don't feel so bad. I've just got an awfully sore penis."

"Well, let's take a look at it." I helped loosen Uncle's pants, unzipped them, and pulled the elastic band of his jockey shorts out far enough so Dr. Morita could take a good look. His scrutiny just took a couple of minutes and then he turned from Uncle, saying to me, "You were right, Gary. You needed to bring him in. We'll have to put him in the hospital and get this problem cleared up. I'll want to get Dr. Skeeters; you know him, don't you?"

"Yes," I replied. "His specialty is urology. I feel bad that I didn't catch this problem before it got to this stage," I apologized.

"This sort of thing happens, Gary, and you shouldn't blame yourself. Do you think he'll mind being admitted into the hospital?" Dr. Morita added in a low voice.

"I don't think he'll mind a bit," I replied.

He then leaned over to uncle and said, "Uncle Charlie, we'll need to admit you into the hospital to get that swelling and soreness cleared up. Are you going to mind?"

"Certainly not," declared Uncle.

With obvious relief, Dr. Morita explained the admitting procedure to me and had Jeannine call over and make sure they had a bed waiting for us. I zipped Uncle back up and followed Dr. Morita out through the examining room door down the hall to the nurse's desk. There, after a few last minute instructions, I was handed a slip of paper with some additional information and told where I was to take

Uncle. I was grateful that the office was so close to the hospital. All I had to do was wheel Uncle down the hill through the emergency room's automatically-opening doors to the front desk of the hospital. There they told me which floor and wing he'd be on and allowed me to take him up there – as long as I promised to come right back and fill out all the inevitable paperwork.

Minutes away from the doctor's office, I had Uncle on the floor in the wing he was to spend two of the last four weeks of his life. The first person who'd come to assist me was Mary, a friend of Judi's from her nursing days at Meridian Park Hospital. She took one look at me and then Uncle and said with unbridled excitement, "This has got to be Uncle Charlie!" She rushed over and put her arms around Uncle, giving him a hearty squeeze as she asked me, "What's wrong!" I stumbled over the explanation, again feeling guilty for allowing this sort of problem to develop. Mary immediately put me at ease, and I helped her get Uncle into his assigned room, undressed and gowned. Uncle's third-floor, private room was on the west wing of the hospital lit by a huge picture window overlooking the yet-undeveloped former cow-pasture grounds. Beyond the empty field you could see the apartments, condos, and portions of the several housing developments that we'd come by only minutes before. The room itself was pie-shaped, with the leading point- the part in an actual piece of pie that the filling usually falls out of – having been cut off to allow room for a door. The architectural design of the building consisted of a series of three-storied round towers. Nursing stations were the hub of each floor, surrounded by single patient rooms pushed up against the outer tower wall.

Uncle's room had an electrically-adjustable bed with stainless steel side rails and was positioned up against the left wall. An I.V. pole stuck straight up on the right side of the headboard and directly behind and above the bed, on the wall was a half dozen valves and gauges for everything from oxygen to emergency monitoring equipment. On the opposite wall hung a small white sink with large faucet handles that could be turned off with the elbows. To the right of the sink was a door that led to the compact yet fully-equipped bathroom. A night stand, the adjustable table, especially designed to slide under and over the bed for serving meals and providing a surface with easy patient access to amenities like tissue and a water glass, and a single chair rounded out the contents of the room.

I felt another twinge of guilt when Mary first saw Uncle's genital area. "It's pretty bad, isn't it?" I said. She put me at ease again, though I knew by her facial expression that his condition was worse than she'd expected.

"We'll get it all cleared up," she assured me. "I've seen worse. A catheter has been ordered, and once he's in bed and that's done, and he's put on some antibiotics, we'll be able to clear it up."

Once Uncle was safely in bed, I told him I'd be back after filling out the papers and left for the admitting desk. I was able to take care of it quickly – by now I was getting good at it – and in about fifteen minutes was back at Uncle's side. He looked cozy and comfortable. The head of the bed slightly raised, covers tucked under his chin, he seemed perfectly relaxed, ready to drop off to sleep.

Dr. Skeeters, who may have been called in from his first love, a ranch in Sherwood, had arrived, Mary informed me, and after several attempts, some anxious moments, and a minimal amount of discomfort, had gotten the catheter in and the prescribed antibiotics were now dripping into a vein from an I.V. bottle hanging above Uncle's bed. I briefly visited with Uncle, who by now wasn't in a talking mood, and then told him I'd be back tomorrow.

12

A TRUE FRIEND KNOWS YOU WELL BUT LIKES YOU ANYWAY

Before leaving the hospital, I telephoned Ruth, Uncle's devoted second cousin, to inform her of the day's events. She accepted the news calmly, thanked me profusely for all I'd done and for keeping her posted, and promised she'd be over to see him the next day. Both she and Esther, her sister, kept coming at least every other day the whole time Uncle was in the hospital. Indeed, they were always more than relatives to Uncle, more like very good old friends who sensed that his time was short and they had better grab every moment that was left 'til the last slipped away.

Uncle had had many friends in his lifetime, but almost all had long since gone to their reward. One dear friend, however, was to "come back" from the 1920's to greet him in a most unusual way. Elenbass Dairy Supply sold a milk tank that was manufactured by a many-faceted, multi-million-dollar equipment company in Madison, Wisconsin. The name of the company is DEC Co., which used to stand for Dairy Equipment Company before they diversified into nondairy fields. Periodically, as happens to all companies, DEC has staff changes. The last time they hired some new employees and switched around some of the old, Mike Ross, a good friend of mine and Uncle's, left to go into business for himself. DEC moved up Mort Mortinson, an older gentleman from California, to take his place. Life on the road, living out of a suitcase, and being away from his young family forced Mike to make a move a bit before he'd planned to, and we sadly said goodbye, wishing him much success.

Not very many weeks into his new assignment, the older factory representative rode along with uncle and me to make a few calls. It turned out that this wasn't his first time in the area; in fact, many years earlier he'd even had his own business in the Northwest and his initial position with DEC Co. had been part of our territory. I introduced Uncle to the 62-year-old and joked that when Uncle went to that great golden dairy farm in the sky (which naturally would have the 40,000 gallon tank Uncle kept talking about) that he could inherit Uncle's seat beside me. In the exchange of introductions, Uncle said, "Mortinson? I used to know a fella named Mortinson."

"Oh, yah?" said the rep.

"Yes," said Uncle. "It was when I lived in Tacoma."

"Oh, really!" said the rep, beginning to take a bit more interest in the conversation. "That's where I grew up. What was his first name?"

"Martin," replied Uncle, without so much as a "Well, let me think."

"That's funny," exclaimed the rep. "That was my father's name, too. What did your friend do?"

"Oh, he was a longshoreman," was Uncle's immediate reply.

On and on went the exchange, with Uncle answering each question with the exact information on the details of the rep's father's job, down even to the physical description of the Tacoma area in which he'd lived. In almost total disbelief, the rep heard Uncle talk about a little boy that Martin often had with him.

At this point, almost bursting with excitement, Mort said to Uncle, "Do you know who that little boy was?"

"No, why?" said Uncle.

"It was me!" said Mort, "And your good friend was my father."

"You?" said Uncle. "Well, I do declare, I do declare."

Over sixty years had passed, and Uncle's close friend had been gone for over twenty-five, but he reached out to us that day in a most unusual way. Chance? As Uncle would say, "Are you crazy?"

Speaking of old friends, there were two older brothers named Fritz and Emal who, I'm sure, ran the only dairy in history on pure love. They were two of my favorite customers. Fritz never married, but Emal had, and his union resulted in two daughters. Though the youngest daughter had an outside job, both pulled their share of the work around the farm. It was no wonder, for their mother set the example, working much harder than most men I'd seen, and at the same time wearing a perpetual smile. They did everything according to the old-day standards, which usually meant more time and effort. No parlor contained them, but rather a rambling, flat barn with stalls build for small Jerseys instead of today's larger, more popular breeds like Fritz and Emal's overfed, well-groomed Holstein "pets."

To make life a bit more comfortable for the biggest cows, they had made wooden, removable covers that fit over the gutters in behind the cows, so when they stood up, they had their back feet on the wood instead of in the gutter itself. Each cow had her own name, and each would have made the proverbial contented cow look cantankerous. Even though I was told by the local creamery's field man that the brothers could afford to put a new tank behind every tree on their well-forested farm they elected to stay with the first and only tank they were ever to buy. This decision cost them plenty, for the creamer had raised the extra-stop charges to the point that a new tank time payment plan would have amounted to much less.

Uncle had had the grandest of times being shown the barn and cows by these two farmers, who weren't that far from being his contemporaries. They'd always invite us in for coffee and cake after my latest attempt to sell them a new tank had crumbled into ruins. On one such occasion, they kept offering more cake, cookies, and the like until Uncle had stuffed down as much as he possibly could. Not wanting to pass up the opportunity this generosity afforded, he began stuffing goodies into his pocket. Carried away by the excitement of the moment, Uncle even picked up some silverware and into the pocket it went.

A few weeks after Uncle's death, I dropped by to see the brothers. I drove down the last mile of the gravel road, and just before I came to their driveway, I noticed a pickup truck sitting just off the road next to the dairy's mailbox. I drove up beside it and lo and behold there sat Emal. He was gazing with a long, sad face at the home place, with its solid buildings and the other improvements mostly built by his father and mother before him. I got out, and Emal told me through the rolled-down window of the events of the last few months. The Grim Reaper had claimed Fritz. He'd had an arthritic condition that left his joints enlarged and fingers gnarled, but a heart condition finally took him. Not long after Fritz's death, Emal had had surgery on his legs to prevent totally losing his ability even to shuffle about. With all these problems, there soon wasn't enough time and "person power" to keep the dairy, with its old-fashioned labor-intensive systems, going. All the cows, pets really, had to be sold and, to add insult to injury, the guy who brought them told Emal that most of them were too old and fat for dairy use and were destined for the slaughterhouse.

Of course, time marches on accompanied by the change and the pain that so often accompany it. But time also eases and then erases that pain as the baton of responsibility and productivity is passed to the next generation. We of that generation must be careful to remember those who have gone and are going. I really need to stop by soon and see Emal and his family.

In talking about old friends, it seems appropriate to mention some of Uncle's attachment to our chief means of transportation. I'm referring, of course, to our beige and brown 1978 Volare. The car really wasn't that old (less than three years when Uncle passed away) but it already had clocked about 130,000 miles. That burden made it much older than its years. Whenever anybody saw a 1978, four-door Volare in Oregon or Southern Washington, I'm just sure they expected to see two people in it, that dairy salesman, old what's his name, and the delightful Uncle Charlie. Uncle loved the car so much that he said it was "almost as good as the long list of great Pontiacs I've had." As could be expected, one day around 100,000 miles, the Volare had to go in for some major rear-end surgery. We were given a loaner which surprisingly wasn't all that bad. Uncle, however, could never get comfortable. He complained about the seat being too low, that the engine didn't really have much pep and, to top everything else, the interior didn't smell right. Really, it did smell "right", and for Uncle that made it wrong.

Finally, almost a week later, the garage called saying that our car was now ready. Uncle and I wasted little time rushing to Meyer Brothers in Newberg to reclaim our "pet". I pulled alongside it and then went to settle our account and pick up the keys. By the time I got back, Uncle was out of the loaner and impatiently waiting by "his" door. He was more than ready to be reunited with his car. I unlocked his door and assisted him into his seat. I then hastily transferred our few things from the loaned vehicle, then jumped in and took off. It felt good! It must have been rather like a cowpoke back astride his favorite horse that's just gotten over a lame leg. But even my satisfaction was nothing compared to the joy of my "Jerriatric" sidekick. There were actual tears streaming down his cheeks, and he kept repeating, "Thank you, Lord. Thank you, Lord."

Neither friendship nor Uncle need be old to be good. Judi's dad and his new wife (she's just a couple of years our senior) came for a visit. Uncle and my father-in-law hit it off right from the start; however, my youthful stepmother-in-law didn't fare quite so well. I introduced Uncle to Barbara, explaining her new relationship to Henry, my father-in-law. Uncle squinted his eyes, peered over his glasses, and said, "Pleased to meet you," and in the same breath, "but I like Yudi the best." Later in the week, we went to the airport to pick up my father-in-law and Barbara, who were coming back from a quick trip up into Canada. Uncle had decided to stay home, but just before we left, he gave us some explicit instructions, "Say, don't let Henry drink too many beers before he gets home. I want to talk to him, and I want him to make sense."

On another occasion on our rounds, Uncle and I stopped in at the Roth dairy. It's near Orchards, a small town just north of Vancouver, Washington. I never did sell George anything, but knowing that perseverance often prevails, my strategy was to keep coming back. Besides, Mrs. Roth was an excellent cook with something always cooling on the kitchen counter and a bottomless pot of coffee brewed to wash it all down. This time I found George out in the barn standing beside his 5,000 gallon milk tank. Unfortunately, it would be awhile before he'd need a bigger one. He greeted me first and said, "Hello," and then, before I could respond, said, "Is Grandpa with you?"

"Grandpa isn't," I replied, "but my Great Uncle Charlie is."

"That's who I mean," he replied. "Come here! With that he hurriedly led me out to another part of his barn and with barely controlled excitement introduced me to a young woman. She was dressed like any of his hired hands but had startling fair skin and blonde, short hair that wasn't so typical.

"Gary, I want you to meet Gro Randly from Norway. I want her to meet Grandpa, I mean Uncle."

On our quick trip out to the car, George explained how he had met Gro on a dock in Puget Sound near Seattle. Gro and two friends had just completed kayaking the Inland Passage to Alaska and were now looking for a way to earn enough money to take a trip down to Costa Rica. Her friends had found work but Gro hadn't. George, after explaining the type of work his hired hands did, offered her a job which she promptly accepted. She'd been there for a couple of months and was already a part of the family. With George's friendliness and his wife's cooking, I'll bet that happened in the first week. By the time he finished his account, we were out to the car and I was trying to get Uncle to roll down the window. I finally gave up and just opened the door and left it open. I bent close to Uncle's ear and introduced him to Gro.

"She's from Norway," I said.

"Yeah?" said Uncle.

With complete understanding as to Uncle's limited hearing ability, Gro leaned down and, speaking directly into his ear, introduced herself in Norwegian. Uncle, who usually takes everything pretty much in stride, whipped his head around to get a look at the person from whom flowed the familiar language of his youth. It must have brought back memories over ninety years old! They talked and talked, Uncle leaning out of the half open car door and Gro bent over to meet him the rest of the way. After fifteen to twenty minutes, with Gro on one side and me on the other, we walked into Mrs. Roth's kitchen where we all, and especially Uncle, munched the Norwegian sweet bread that Gro had baked, drank coffee, and sampled a dark brown Norwegian sweet cheese that only Gro and Uncle really seemed to enjoy. I finally had to break up the party to head for other dairies, hopefully ones ready to buy from us. But none could be as hospitable as the one we were about to leave.

One friend of Uncle's was literally an old goat. He had come to us years earlier when I had co-owned a light metal fabrication stove manufacturing business. My partner Eldon Schnell suggested we get a goat to keep down the grass around our shop. The city of Sherwood had gotten after us for this unsightly problem several times, and the goat sounded like just the solution. I didn't waste any time putting the idea into action. Within forty-eight hours, I'd located and purchased a young white billy goat. To mark the occasion of having him castrated, I christened him Hannibal (or Had-a-ball, if you say it slow). Then I brought him to the shop and showed him to Eldon, saying, "How do you like our new goat?"

He smiled grimly. "What do you mean 'our' goat? You bought him, he's yours."

"I thought you said what we needed around here was a goat to keep the grass down?" I countered.

"I did," said Eldon. "But I really didn't mean it. You won't believe the trouble one of those critters can get you into."

I looked down at the cute, wee white wad of fur and wondered how anyone in his right mind could make such an accusation. However, Hannibal was still too small to start in on our grass, so I ended up taking him home for Cathi and Berniece to fight over who got to feed and care for him. No goat ever had it so good. The girls found a nipple and pop bottle and fed him warmed milk, snuggled up in a blanket in their arms.

Hannibal grew fast and was soon bouncing around outside our house, playing and sleeping with our two little dogs. He could climb anything and always had the cutest look on his face when he'd bounce up onto the hood of our car just as Judi drove in after a hard day's work, peering lovingly through the windshield at her. For some reason Judi didn't share in the adoration of this beautiful little creature's cute ways. I suppose part of the reason was that Judi no longer could sunbathe on the decks. Hannibal, who considered himself part human, couldn't stand to leave any of us alone when we were outside. The last time Judi tried getting some rays, Hannibal rushed up and lovingly nudged her a few times. Really his horns weren't as sharp as Judi said, and she'd probably cut herself shaving earlier. But I agreed it was rotten of him to pee all over her feet, even though it was just from happiness at seeing her. Anyway, Judi had really gotten mad, even calling me at work ranting that something had to be done with Hannibal. It's strange how some people just don't care for animals.

Not many days later, all of us piled into the car and went down to the park to play a little tennis. We had a lovely time, stopping for a treat at the corner store before arriving home about three hours later. As usual, I was the first one out of the car and, anxious to raid the refrigerator, Berniece wasn't far behind me. We came in the downstairs door, and I started up the spiral stairs. I got half way up to the middle floor, to the point where I could look down through the railings at our breathtaking living room. Judi's an excellent amateur interior decorator, one who could put many professionals to shame. Our living room includes a lovely white L-shaped designer couch with loose cushion backs and several hundred dollars' worth of hand-made pillows. They'd all been individually picked from a number of some of Portland's finest shops. Nestled in the crook of the L is a chrome contemporary four-and-one-half-foot-square coffee table with a plate glass top. It sits over the top of a real zebra-skin rug with its neck and mane sticking out one end, the tail out the other, and the legs out both sides. A matching chrome library table with a mirrored top, complete with a handmade, clear-globed lamp resting on it with a tasteful array of pictures in cute little free-standing frames is positioned behind the longest part of the couch. This complete arrangement is facing a turn-of-the-century, original hard-coal-base-burning parlor stove that, with its nine doors, forty pieces of nickel-plated brick-brack and filigreed crown, looks like something out of a Far Eastern temple. The rest of the room consists of banks of picture windows, two sliding glass doors on either side for access to the spacious decks, and about seven plants, several being six or eight feet high. We don't spend much time in the erroneously-named "living" room, preferring to maintain it as the one room that always looks nice for unexpected company.

Well, at least almost always. My glance at the normally House Beautiful's front-cover-quality room usually brought a thrill; this time it produced a chill. There, standing jauntily on the zebra-skin rug between the couch and coffee table, house-plant greenery still hanging from each side of his mouth, was Hannibal.

I froze, and Berniece slammed right into me. I blinked, hoping the awful vision would go away and I would awaken from the nightmare. No such luck. The room was a disaster. The lamp was knocked over, the pillows were strewn all over. The six to eight foot plants were either much shorter or had holes eaten through them as high as Hannibal could reach. To make matters worse, piles of goat droppings littered the room. I knew there would be hell to pay by someone, and that someone was me.

I finally unfroze and tried speaking, just to make sure I still could. Once I'd established that fact, I turned to Berniece and told her to get back downstairs. Whatever she did, she wasn't to let her mother come up to the middle floor while I did what I could to clean and straighten up the mess. Maybe she'd never know what happed. Fortunately, several frenzied minutes passed before Judi and Cathi even came in the house, and Berniece, who didn't want to become another of the many offspring of divorced parents, got Judi interested in a Barbara Walters' Special downstairs. I didn't care much for Barbara or her specials, but this time she got me out of an especially tight situation and that's made me one of her most avid fans. Before Judi came in, I was able to get Hannibal out through the partly open screen he'd come through. He must have been scratching himself, rubbing back and forth on the shut screen which slid open enough so that he could push his way in and wreak his havoc. Phew!

Once Hannibal was out, I surveyed the damage more closely. It was worse than I thought. The large plants could be turned or similar ones from other places in the house brought in to replace the destroyed. The scattered pillows could be retrieved, dusted off, and wouldn't look too much the worse for the wear. And, fortunately, goat crap comes in neat pea-sized pieces. Though weeks would pass before the last one was to be disposed of, I could clean up most of them and sweep the rest under the couch or rug. The lamp was a bit bent, but with an artful twist here and there, only I would know that it would never be the same. It doesn't sound too bad, you say? Well, you should have seen the white, L-shaped couch. Hannibal had gotten up on the bench and back of the couch and pissed on every last cushion. He hadn't missed one. I was sick. Judi doesn't get mad very often, but when she does, the explosion more than makes up for the times she doesn't. I knew if she saw this mess, especially the couch, the situation could be worse than all the other times put together.

I must admit, though I didn't approve of Watergate and the way President Nixon handled it, I now really sympathized with the man and felt he did what almost anyone else would do under such circumstances. I feel I attempted the second greatest cover-up in history, second only because the house we live in doesn't happen to be white. Berniece and later Cathi helped, keeping Judi downstairs for about two and a half hours. They brought her coffee and ice cream, and made her popcorn, doing everything possible while I switched, straightened, and picked up, wondering all the while what I was going to do about the yellow-streaked white couch.

Finally, I decided, after restoring everything else to a semblance of normalcy, what I'd do. I would wait until I'd gotten Judi all the way up to our third-floor bedroom and asleep. I'd then sneak down and try to clean the couch. So, after Judi was snoring soundly, which I could keep track of even as I cleaned, since our bedroom is a loft, I quietly made my way downstairs and tackled the chore. For lack of anything else, I used some pink liquid dishwashing soap. I wetted down the cushions and scrubbed until I was totally exhausted. I hope that when they dried, which wasn't going to be for several days, somehow all traces of goat urine would vanish. After flipping the cushions over, wet side down, I went to bed with that hope in mind. The next day, when nobody was looking, I carefully lifted up one of the cushions to see what it looked like. My fears were confirmed; it looked even worse. Not to be caught without another cleaning plan, I figured I'd contact an upholstery cleaner and have them out, while Judi was at work to clean the couch in place.

From this point on, as Judi tells it, she was hardly allowed to step a foot into the house. I took her to dinner, to the movies, shopping, whatever – anything to stall for time until I could get the mess cleaned up. Judi began getting suspicious, even calling her aunt, almost in tears, saying, "Something is wrong with Gary! Either he has a girlfriend and is trying to assuage his guilt, or something else is terribly wrong." After hearing the way I was acting, Aunt Nina agreed that it must be another woman, but did her best to calm Judi down. Though tense, life kept going on a fairly even keel.

Three days after the fateful evening, Judi was bustling about getting ready for a visit from my high school best friend, Mel Kolstad, and his family. They were coming down from Seattle to spend a few days. Judi enjoys her home and, after being in the work force and the rat race that so often surrounds it, just loves to putter around inside the house. This she does smiling and singing, a labor of love for us and herself. However, when company is coming, a whole new Judi emerges. She becomes a drill sergeant, Egyptian taskmaster, and Vince Lombardy all rolled into one. The smile is replaced by a snarl, the song by shrill commands, and we're each, Cathi, Berniece and I, given a list of the chores that are our responsibility. Worst of all, she doesn't believe we'll do it right (or at all) unless she's standing over our shoulders, barking at us.

On this occasion, I was outside carrying out part of my assignment, the girls downstairs cleaning up their rooms and Uncle's area. Judi, on the middle level, moved into the living room and began dusting and fluffing up the pillows when she noticed some dampness. She flipped over a cushion . . . and another, and another, and hollered, "Girls! Get up here right now!" The girls came running and, about half way up the stairs, at the same point I had seen Hannibal three days earlier, came to a screeching halt. There was Judi standing exactly where he'd been, clutching a still-wet, stained cushion. The girls, almost in unison, gasped, "I think we'd better get Dad." With that, they turned and rushed outside after me.

I wasn't far and had heard Judi's yell, well aware that my own personal cover-up was about to be exposed. I came in the house on the first level and began the ascent of the spiral stairs. It seemed as if I were climbing Mt. Everest. Judi later said that I "looked like a puppy dog that knew he was in for a whipping." But just then she was so mad that she could barely see straight. What little she did see was me, my tail between my legs, dragging up the steps. I looked so pathetic that she lost her anger for a few seconds and let a smile slip. I couldn't believe what I'd see (the smile, I mean) and it was just as well, because it didn't last long. She listened to my story and was furious. We all stood there as she recapped how she had worked, slaved, and saved to buy the couch, only to have it ruined by a goat that, if she'd had anything to say about it, we'd never have had in the first place. I explained that I was hoping to get an upholstery-cleaning outfit to come out and clean it in place, but so far hadn't found one.

Saved by the bell! About that time, Mel and his wife, Louise, telephoned and I was able to slip away to escort them to our fairly hard place to find. My trip took about forty-five minutes to get to where the Kolstad's had called from and back home. I wasn't sure what kind of hospitality we'd be providing under the circumstances. When I arrived home with Mel and family following me, I briefly explained that things were in a bit of an upheaval. Mel, who'd raised many goats back home on the farm, just about died laughing. When I finally got them inside, Judi was on the phone. She had located an upholstery cleaner who not only felt he could do the job but who would come out right away. After carefully looking the whole couch over, he took all the soiled cushions with the promise that he'd do the very best job that could be done.

Our visit with Mel and Louise went very well, with the Hannibal incident only brought up occasionally when the conversation lagged a bit. Two weeks and $300 later, we got the cushions back looking almost as good as new. I say "almost" because the guy got every bit of the dirt and urine out but couldn't understand what the pinkish stain was. He had nothing in his arsenal of cleaning chemicals that would touch it. I then showed him what was left of the liquid dishwashing soap, and the color-fast mystery was solved. If I'd only owned up to my mistake, taken my medicine like a man, and let the professionals handle the mess from the start, there'd be no tell-tale stains today. I'll bet Richard Nixon would have agreed with me.

You might think that I would sell, give away, or maybe even murder Hannibal. I didn't. I kept him around just to show that I was in charge, and when enough time had elapsed to make that point, I gave him to a friend who had some blackberries he wanted cleaned out. Several months later, his wife left him. I've always been afraid to ask why.

Though Eldon and I had problems getting along in business together and finally split up, we're still good friends, and I have a great deal of respect for his opinion, especially when it comes to goats' nature. "You won't believe the trouble one of the critters can get you into," he had warned me. Well, Eldon, I'm a believer!

Uncle missed the goat when it was gone, but the only real pleasure he got from it was when he could watch its antics from the safety of inside the house. Outside, as Uncle sat in his favorite chair on the deck in the sun, Hannibal would usually get in the way. He'd butt Uncle; Uncle would poke at him with his cane to drive him off. Hannibal thought this was a game, and before you knew it, the situation would escalate into a duel. Uncle talked to him, just as if he were another part of the family. Several months passed after Hannibal's departure before Uncle stopped asking about him.

Uncle and first wife Gertrude (my mother's mother's sister) in the 1940's

Uncle's Failing Street living room

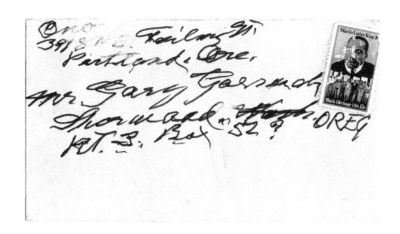

Uncle's formal acceptance of Gary's offer to live with the Gorsuch family

Family dinner in our Sherwood dining room

Dinner at Ruth and Esther's

Uncle, Ruth, Esther, Cathi, and Berniece

Party time at Ruth and Esther's

Uncle and our parlor stove in our Sherwood living room

Uncle checking out our newly purchased Sherwood home

"I can't believe 'Jerry' kept those fish alive."

Judi ("Yudi"), Uncle, Cathi, and Berniece on Ruth and Esther's porch

"Can I trade him in for a Saint Bernard?"
(Uncle seated on his first floor hide-a-bed)

Mick and Johnny just before we used those "cash" tickets

A salesman and his 95-year old story telling uncle

By Clyde List

Every day of the week Gary Gorusch of Sherwood gets into his 1978 Volare and makes his rounds. he sells Clean-Rite Milk Tank Washers, Dari-Kool Farm Milk Coolers, and Therma-Stor Heat Recovery Systems to dairymen as far away as the Yakima Valley, Tillamook, and "points south."

Many office workers would envy a job—and a gift of gab—that would take them through the Oregon countryside, especially at this time of the year. But Gorusch, who has his irons in more than one fire around here (many of us know him as the designer-promoter of the Sherwood stove), has found that being on the road can get a little tedious. Along with all those jokes that farmers tell about traveling salesmen.

But then that was before Uncle Charlie dropped in for a visit. Uncle Charlie is pushing 96 years of age, is slightly hard of hearing but tells a good story. After a few trips into the countryside with his nephew

with. "I don't want you to think I'm trying to take advantage of him," said Gorusch, "but it does help sales when I have him along. Especially when I introduce him to the older farmers."

It is fairly certain that wherever they go to make a sales pitch, they are not soon forgotten. Uncle Charles has seen a great deal in his long life, but he has never seen anything like the modern dairy farm in operation. It is not uncommon for him to look over the premises while Gary is explaining the finer points of his cooling system to a dairyman.

On one occasion Gary was startled in mid-sentence to see a hired hand stagger out of the barn, bent over double as if he had been kicked in the stomach by one of the livestock. He was not dying from a burst appendix, but from laughter. Behind him came Uncle Charlie covered from head to toe with an indelicate substance often found in barnyards.

It seems he had gotten a ...

SHERWOOD SALESMAN GARY GORUSCH and Uncle Charles One set out to conquer the dairy industry. Gary says that his 95 year old uncle is guaran-

teed to turn even the most routine sales presentation into a disaster.   -List photo

mishap out on the farm for the senior salesman. Other stories can be heard in bars or after-

dredging the Willamette River. So maybe it's understandable that a few spills

sentimental about Norway, of raw clams and oysters. As far as "Jerry" is concerned, Uncle Charlie is more

1974 'Sherwood Tribune' article

117

13

EVERYBODY WANTS TO LIVE LONG, BUT NOBODY WANTS TO GET OLD

The next day, before hitting the road to make my rounds, I swung by Meridian Park Hospital to see Uncle. He was doing as well as could be expected. The infection looked about the same but no worse, thank goodness. Though he didn't always know where he was or why he was where he was, he surely did enjoy all the attention the nurses showered upon him. I talked to one nurse who said that, apart from pulling the catheter out once and attempting several other times, he was a good patient and they just loved him. I left after giving Uncle a squeeze and assuring him that a lot of dairymen would be asking where Uncle Charlie was. That comment seemed to perk him up a bit, and as if to confirm my statement, every single customer that day asked about him.

That evening before going home, I swung by to check up on him again. Ruth and Esther had been there earlier, and later that evening, gave me their assessment of his condition. Uncle looked quite good. He'd been bathed and shaved, and I was in the process of seeing if I could get him to recognize me when Dr. Morita walked in. I asked how he felt things were going. He said the infection was under control and would heal nicely, but he expressed concern that Uncle was quite anemic, wasn't eating very well, and showed no interest at all in walking. I explained that this had been true of him before the infection, except for the lack of appetite. Lloyd said that the years were beginning to show, Uncle was tired, and some of his "parts" were nearly worn out. After Dr. Morita left, I stood by Uncle's bed for several minutes reflecting on Uncle's years. He was, except by the ante-deluvian standards, a very, very old man.

To me, Uncle had always been old. He was in his sixties when I was born, almost ready to retire. Even back then, forty years ago, he was pushing the average life span for males. In spite of this fact, Uncle seldom, if ever, considered himself old. I'll never forget the letter he sent back to us when he took his first airplane ride.

In his early nineties he had decided to take a trip to Norway to visit the few family members that remained. Ruth assisted him, making all the arrangements and seeing that he took a proper wardrobe, including a brand new overcoat and dress hat. Uncle allowed her to make all the choices – well, almost. Uncle didn't like the feather in the hat she selected, and the deal wasn't consummated until the astute salesperson switched feathers from hat to hat until he'd found just the right combination. With that and the rest of the preparations complete, the day of departure arrived and Uncle soared off into the clouds. His first letter he sent back read, in part, like this, ". . . had a wonderful flight over. I sat between an over-decorated sea captain and an old lady . . . "

My heart goes out to the old people who have additional hardships heaped upon the already-heavy load of old age. Once in a while, Uncle would waver under the burden, especially when he felt concerned about his eyesight.

"I can't see, I can't see," he'd say, his voice shaking. "I'm totally blind in this eye," pointing to his left, "and can barely see out of the right. Let me tell you, getting old is no fun."

Fortunately, he didn't allow that depressing thought to stay in his conscious mind for long. A few minutes later he'd respond to someone asking how he was feeling with an "I couldn't feel better. I always feel the same. The Lord has been good to me." Indeed, the Lord had been good to him, but the natural laws that his Lord had set in place were beginning to gain the upper hand. Solomon described the situation perfectly when he encouraged people to forget not their Creator in their younger years when the temptation is to neglect God and "do your own thing." In Ecclesiastes 12 he wrote, "Remember your Creator in the days of your youth, before the days of trouble come and the years approach when you will say, 'I find no pleasure in them . . .', when the keepers of the house (hands) tremble, and the strong men (legs) stoop, when the grinders (teeth) cease because they are few, and those looking through the window (eyes) grow dim, when the doors of the street (lips) are closed and the sound of grinding (digestion) fades, when men rise up at the sound of birds (insomnia), but all their songs grow faint (hard of hearing); when men are afraid of heights (loss of equilibrium), and of dangers in the streets (loss of security); when the almond tree blossoms (bitterness emerges) and the grasshopper drags himself along (weakness) and desire no longer is stirred (loss of sexual desire)."

Uncle, though more stubborn at certain times than anyone I've known, hadn't forgotten his Creator in the days of his youth, and as a result, I'm convinced he was better able to take the hardships and discomforts of growing old than anyone I've known or heard about.

Call it pride, independence, or whatever, but Uncle refused to use even a cane until the last three or four years of his life. I don't think the concession would have come that soon except that he had seen my grandfather, O.B. Hauge, who had been having leg problems (both had to be amputated before his death) using a cane. His son, my Uncle Johnny, had made a cane for him, carefully fashioning it out of a piece of half-inch metal electrical conduit.

After returning to Portland from a visit to my parents' home in Ferndale, Washington, where my grandfather was living, Uncle asked me if I could make him a cane like O.B.'s. I said "Sure," and proceeded to do my thing with the same type of material. Using heat from a small propane torch, I carefully formed a crook. And then, following Uncle Johnny's lead, wrapped and rewrapped the handle with black electrical tape. I finished the project by capping off the ground end with a rubber cane tip. When I presented the finished product to Uncle, his response was more than payment for the time, effort and materials I had used in its construction. You'd have thought I'd given Uncle a million dollars!

He used that cane a year or two before coming to live with us full time. When he moved in, I finally decided, with all the places we went and people we met, he needed something that didn't look so homemade. I went out and bought him a nice wooden one, but do you think Uncle was grateful or would use it? Of course not. My solution to that problem was one day, accidentally on purpose, Uncle's metal conduit cane got lost. It's still stashed behind our freezer in a downstairs cubbyhole. But months elapsed before he finally quit asking if I'd ever come across "my good metal cane, the one with the black tape on the handle." I felt guilty each time he asked, and more than once I almost went over to its hiding place to bring it to him.

However, Uncle's cane wasn't always enough to give his body the support it needed. For the two years he lived with us, up until the last couple of months, he'd come up the spiral stairs a couple of times a day. Able-bodied people a third his age had problems with the tight-turning, pie-shaped treads, but not Uncle. He'd hook his cane over the right arm going up and the left arm coming down. He'd then grab the outside railing (the one the girls simply slide down) with one hand and the center post that went all the way to the top with the other. When he got to the landing, he would disengage the cane from the crook of his arm and be ready to head off. If he had been on his way upstairs, that usually meant he was hungry. He'd round the corner off the landing to the right, proceed down the hall and past the kitchen on the left. This is where the wall on the right stopped, opening up into the living room. Dead ahead was the dining room. On the way, he'd lean his hand against the wall as he moved along. Once he got to the end of the wall, there wasn't anything for him to lean on except the cane. The last few times he made this trip, he'd stand at this point and holler," Would someone come and give me their elbow?" One of us would rush to help him over to his chair at the dining room table. Otherwise, when he reached the end of the wall, he would launch himself out into the no-support area, at first rocking from toe to heel until he got his balance; then, leaning forward as if into a strong wind, he'd strike out for the dining room and his chair. Once safe in his chair, he would grab the lower lip of the table and with a minimal amount of help from his feet pull himself and the chair with a screech as close to the table as he could get.

He'd then start shouting his orders, "Coffee!" or "Toast and coffee!" or "Soup, bread, and coffee! For a while all he wanted were pork chops. After getting served and eating and drinking his fill, he'd push back away from the table with another screech like a person dragging his fingernails across a blackboard. Try as we might with everything from heavy felt glued to the chair-leg bottoms to socks secured over the legs, the solutions for that spine-chilling screech were short-lived. Back he'd scoot, often needing some help to get up out of his chair. Then he would zig-zag across the open space to the support area down the hall, which again he leaned up against as he walked along. To the day of this writing, we can still see the mark along the otherwise white wall where Uncle brushed in all of his coming and going. It's a perfectly straight line waist high the full length of the hall wall. He'd then repeat the process he used coming up the stairs, only in reverse going down. Once downstairs he'd either call for assistance to get over to his chair or go into the toe to heel routine and somehow make the last fifteen feet from landing to chair with simply his cane.

Despite his age and infirmities Uncle came with me to the 1981 Oregon State Dairy Convention in Eugene, Oregon. I was manning our eight-foot display table, promoting the products we sold. He sat to my right, stiff-legged, toes up, heels down, hands clasped across his lap. His cap and spectacles were fixed in place, cane clenched between his legs, and his chin resting comfortable on his chest, sound asleep. A young dairyman walked by, stopped, turned around and with a straight face said, "So that's what I'll look like with all the stress and strain of dairy life, at age forty." Though people made many different remarks about Uncle, everyone treated him with a great deal of respect and admiration. The words of Moses in Leviticus 19:32 come to mind, "Rise in the presence of the aged, show respect for the elderly, and revere your God . . . "(N.I.V.). This sentiment was expressed by the actions and attitudes of most all with whom Uncle came in contact, especially those in the dairy industry.

14

PATIENCE IS BITTER, BUT ITS FRUIT IS SWEET

Before Dr. Morita left Uncle's bedside, he answered several more of my questions. He said they'd get the urinary tract cleared up and then they would turn their attention to his other problems. I stayed awhile longer, trying to get Uncle to recognize me, but my efforts were futile. Senility, I've been told, is the most common word applied to this behavior in older people, but I've always preferred to refer to Uncle's spells simply as times of forgetfulness or confusion.

Speaking of confusion, the first year Uncle was with us, he didn't want to miss a thing, so he went with us every place we'd go. One weekend evening, Judi was working, so we decided to take in a movie we knew she wouldn't be interested in. Though later in our life with Uncle we were able to leave him at home for a few hours and get away with it, his response to "Would you like to take in a show tonight, Uncle?" was a "Why, sure!" So off we went to the Joy Theater in downtown Tigard. It was a blood-and-guts, suspense-horror thriller called "Invasion of the Body Snatchers." Uncle stayed awake through the whole thing, with his only overt reaction being an occasional smile and inappropriately-timed chuckle. After it was over, we shuffled out of the theater at Uncle's slow but steady pace, finally making it to the car.

"How did you like the movie?" one of the girls asked.

"Great," said Uncle. "It was one of the best comedies I've ever seen."

I quickly glanced over to see if he was "pulling our legs," but I could see that he was giving his honest evaluation of the film. Not being able to hear or see too well had completely turned around the filmmakers' desired horrific effect.

On another movie outing we weren't so lucky. Uncle understood only too well the plot of the picture and apparently took it personally. We, Judi included this time, happily headed off to what we thought was a film Uncle would really enjoy, George Burns and Walter Matthau in the "Sunshine Boys." All except Uncle laughed our way through the entire show. Many times we nudged one another as a scene or behavior trait perfectly mirrored the way Uncle lived or behaved. Walter's apartment looked like Uncle's, and the way he cooked was a dead ringer for Uncle's style. However, no laughter came from Uncle that day, and when we left the theater and asked Uncle what he thought of the picture, all we got was a grunt and, "I really didn't care for it at all." The next time "The Invasion of the Body Snatchers" is in town, I think I'll take another look at it. I may really have missed something.

As the above story may indicate, Uncle wasn't the only one who got confused. One occasion which at first had me confused was the late fall day we looped around the Tillamook Valley. We were coming around the corner near the Christenson dairy when I noticed the most unusual-looking herd of Jersey cows I'd ever seen. The closer we got to the herd, the more confused I became. Soon they were so near, it seemed we could reach out and touch them. Then it suddenly dawned on me. "Uncle," I cried, "look at the elk!" I pulled off the road and stopped. It took only seconds for Uncle to focus in on them. "Boy, oh boy," was all he could say. We relished every second, enjoying the beauty and grace of about twenty of the most magnificent coastal elk I'd ever seen grazing in the pasture alongside the road. They were only a few yards away from us, and we stayed until they got a bit nervous and moved on. Uncle never forgot that experience, even though he didn't remember what to call them. He usually referred to them as "antelopes" and multiplied their numbers several times over. Almost without fail, regardless of the time of year, whenever in Tillamook, he'd suggest we loop around the valley and see if we could spot "that herd of antelopes."

A couple of other times, someone else was confused, not Uncle, which showed me that lots of people out there are willing to get involved. We just always hear about the few who are idly standing by while someone drowns, is raped, or is murdered.

One winter evening, I had a late appointment at the Ramada Inn in Tualatin. Uncle, of course, was along but didn't want to come in. I went out periodically to check on him and would start the car up for short periods of time to make sure Uncle stayed warm. During one of the times the engine was running, I heard a page asking that the owner of beige Volare, license number such-and-such, please come to the front desk. "Oh, no!" I gasped, and didn't even excuse myself, other than saying I'd be right back. Instead of going to the front desk, I dashed straight out to the car. Upon reaching the car, I threw open the door, not knowing quite what to expect.

Uncle awoke with a start, demanding angrily, "What do you want?"

"Nothing," I said, "Just checking to see that you're all right."

"Well, my goodness!" he complained. "You could be a little more gentle about it!"

"I'm sorry, Uncle. Not much longer and we'll be ready to leave."

"Take your time, take your time. I'm in no hurry," said Uncle.

Making sure everything else was fine and that he'd be warm and comfortable for the next several minutes, I shut off the engine and went back inside. I stopped by the desk to talk to the manager, who said that another patron had come by the car and, seeing Uncle slumped in the seat with his chin on his chest and the motor running, became concerned for Uncle's safety and contacted the manager. I thanked him for his concern, concluded the remainder of my appointment without incident, and Uncle and I hit the road again.

A similar incident of confusion occurred at the University Hospital parking lot in downtown Portland. I had left Uncle while visiting my brother, Charlie, who was in the hospital for some more chemotherapy for his cancer. I'd left the engine running again, as it was a very cold day. It seems that a student happened by, as best I could later figure out from Uncle's account, and banged on the window.

"He said something about affixiation, I don't exactly know what he was talking about," explained Uncle. "But whatever it was, I hope he gets over it."

Nothing seemed to please my customers more than showing

Uncle around their farms. One person who was no exception was Joe Fugundes. He led Uncle into one of the four rooms in the long building where he raises veal. He then took Uncle by the arm and they walked down in front of about sixty calves (only a few of the over two hundred calves that he was raising at the time). Bawling calves lined both sides of the room. Uncle moved off on his own, pausing every few feet to scratch a head or two before moving a bit farther down the line. Joe and I visited while Uncle inspected the calves. He couldn't fully express his awe. He stopped, leaned on his cane, saying his often repeated words, "Boy, oh boy! Boy, oh boy!" In the weeks and months that followed, whenever he spotted a calf he'd launch into his account of the "Portagee fella in the valley" and his "thousands of veal calves."

In the outskirts of Washington's Centralia, on the Bower dairy, Uncle was given a similar experience to add to his growing list of sights on the farm. A couple dozen Ayrshire heifers in various stages of growth were lined up along one side of their barn. Butch and Glen, with Slim, their father (a nickname carried over from his leaner days), showed Uncle their prize winning stock. For weeks, Uncle would say to dairymen, many who had several times more stock than the Bowers, "If you want to see the best looking herd of heifers there is, you ought to go up – where was that place, Jerry?"

"Centralia, Uncle."

"Ya, Centralia. There are some boys up there that really know how to do it, and they got hundreds of them. But they won't sell a one, so it'll do no good to ask them." Hundreds it wasn't, but they were very nice animals and they brought Uncle immeasurable pleasure.

131

Since the majority of our business concerned milk tanks, and since Uncle considered himself as much if not more a part of the operation as anyone, he threw himself into it with real enthusiasm. His poor eyesight, however, got him once into a pile of manure out of which we both emerged smelling like the proverbial roses. I'd heard about Herman DeMattas, a new dairyman in the Nehalem area who'd come up from Modesto, California. He had purchased the Hurliman place at the north end of the valley and had decided to increase his herd. This spelled "new tank" so big and bold that I couldn't get over to see him fast enough. Set off the road about three-fourths of a mile, the buildings on the DeMattas dairy are clustered together in the center of the farm. Behind the white frame house looms a large hip-roofed barn and cluster of three silos. There's a good sized equipment shed to the left of the barn, with a much larger loafing shed to the right. On the house side of the barn is a sturdy milk house with poured-cement walls stout enough to serve as a bomb shelter.

Uncle and I arrived and, after introducing ourselves to Herman, I set about the task of selling him a new tank. Since Herman is Portuguese and so is Judi's father's side of the family, and since they were raised in the same part of California, we immediately seemed to hit it off. Conveniently, just down the road lived Orv and Walt Porter, whom I'd sold a tank to several months before. I took Herman to see their tank. If it proved necessary, I could also take him to the Larry and Blake Meyers' dairy a mile or so further down the road. I'd also sold them a tank a while before I'd sold one to the Porters. That sale had taken me about eight months and over thirty calls.

After our visit with Walt, who we'd caught out in the woods

cutting a cord or two of their winter's wood, we headed back to Herman's dairy for the final nudge toward a first-call sale. I parked the car and Herman and I went into the milk house, leaving Uncle seated comfortably in his front seat. We discussed the size he'd need, based on the numbers of cows he'd be milking, and I measured the milk house and discussed his trade. I was able to quote him a price and assure him that the balance could be financed through the Tillamook County Creamery (a co-op that he, as a milk shipper, was part owner of and which had a number of good programs to assist its members).

Tillamook Creamery is an extremely successful producer of the finest cheddar cheese in the world. This achievement is due to the unique conditions of Tillamook County – its lush grassy fields, mild climate, and the careful quality-control procedures enforced by their field man, Duane Brown, and flavor specialist, Tom Baily, and their staffs. They sample each producer's shipment by tasting, smelling, and conducting a number of technical tests. They also taste all batches of cheese, selling off anything that doesn't measure up to the highest standards in the industry. Because of this process, they demand and get some of the highest prices for their product in the country. This, in turn, is passed back to the dairyman in the form of higher prices for their milk and special services like the tank-financing program Herman could take advantage of.

My presentation had been flawless, and Herman was ready to wrap his fingers around my pen and become happily involved with a brand-new Elenbaas milk tank. In triumph, I glanced out towards the car before offering Herman my pen. Suddenly I forgot all about the sale. The car door gaped open; Uncle was gone. A rush of air and a groan escaped my mouth together.

"What's wrong?" Herman asked.

"It's Uncle," I said. "He's gotten out of the car."

We both rushed out into the barnyard driveway. I quickly looked around. Then I ran over to the car, but Uncle wasn't lying on the seat out of sight from where we'd been, or lying on the ground near the half-opened door. I spotted some machinery and hustled over to it. To my relief, there was Uncle. He had fallen into a big puddle of mud and manure. Cane still in his right hand, feet slightly spread in front of him, Uncle Lay on his back partially propped up on his left elbow and forearm. Fortunately, the puddle wasn't more than two or three inches deep. The expression of rueful chagrin on Uncle's face was what you'd expect to find on a kid who'd been caught with his hand in the cookie jar.

My first reaction was concern that he hadn't hurt himself. As is so often the case with a parent and an erring child, once you've discovered he's all right, your concern changes to anger. That emotion only lasted long enough for me to tell Uncle in no uncertain terms that he shouldn't get out and wander around dairies. He could really be badly injured. However, once through with the tongue-lashing, my anger, and with Herman's help I assisted Uncle back to the car, was replaced by a new fear – fear that I would lose my opportunity to close the sale. Carefully, with Herman under one arm and me under the other, we propped a bedraggled Uncle up against the side of the Volare. Mud and manure dripped off of him, with more than a little getting on the both of us.

"Why did you leave the car, Uncle?" I asked.

"Oh," muttered Uncle, still not in full voice and obviously still shaken, "I saw that milk tank over there and thought I'd have a closer look." Herman and I looked in the direction he motioned. There, bigger than life, stood a several-thousand-gallon liquid manure tank on wheels – the kind dairymen use to hold cow excrement mixed with water for spreading onto their pastures as fertilizer.

Herman and I couldn't help laughing. We tried explaining to Uncle what kind of tank it was as we scraped as much of the muck off him as we could. He felt bad enough having fallen, and I believe we made matters worse when he finally understood what kind of tank he'd gone to check out. We did what we could to clean him up, and with Herman saying over and over again, "Are you sure you're all right? I've got insurance," we got him back to the car. I wasn't sure now what kind of deal could be salvaged, and I even weighed the possibility of leaving right then and planning to come back another day to try to make the sale. But to be this close and not at least to attempt a close would be a salesman's unpardonable sin. So, acting as if pulling Uncle out of a pile of manure was an everyday occurrence, I moved into an assumed close.

"Well, Herman, could you be ready for your new tank in three weeks?" I ventured. And then I waited.

I didn't have to wait long, for if he hadn't been ready to buy before Uncle's plunge into the puddle he was now. Whether wanting to be as agreeable as possible lest we come back and sue for unsafe barnyard conditions, which we'd never have done, or for some other reason, he said, "Three weeks? Sure."

Without a single wasted moment, I whipped out a contract and minutes later Uncle and I were headed down the highway with (at least on this day) the pleasant smell of moo manure mixing with the odor of drying ink on our one-stop-and-a-sale contract.

A similar experience happened on the John and Sharon Seaman's dairy north of the DeMattas place near Brownsmede. I stopped by on a normal post installation visit to check that all was working well with the tank our crew had recently installed. Sharon was in the parlor milking, and after a brief exchange on how things were going, I asked if she'd mind if I brought Uncle in to take a look. It would be the very first milk parlor he'd ever seen. "Why, sure," agreed Sharon.

Out I went and brought back Uncle, who became captivated and amazed by what he saw. He stood immobile for several minutes watching Sharon, the cows, the milking machines, and all the activity accompanying the normal parlor procedures. Then, wanting to get the most out of the experience, Uncle moved farther into the pit area and up as close to the splash curbing as possible. It was then that Uncle paid the inevitable price for his parlor curiosity. As he tells it, "I got too close to the back end of one of those cows. A Jersey, I believe it was. Well, anyway, it coiled up its tail over its backside and poof! There was shit all over the place. Jerry had to take me outside and turn a hose on me, and that didn't even get it all off me. Boy, oh boy! Boy, oh boy!"

The pants we could wash, but try as we might to sponge and spot his wool jacket in the days that followed, we finally gave up and sneaked it off to the cleaners, rolled up with the outside in, hidden in the middle of a pile of other clothing, hoping that somehow no one would notice the distinctive smell.

Since we're talking about Tillamook County and some of the ways Uncle got confused, I've got a couple more tales to tell. Once, while visiting a friend in his home, we moved from the kitchen where we, including Uncle, had enjoyed coffee and cake, to the living room, I picked out a chair for Uncle similar to the one he sat in near his bed at home. Here I knew he'd be comfortable and probably doze as we continued our visit. We all got absorbed in our conversation and Uncle was forgotten. Several minutes later, while someone was taking a breath before continuing on, I glanced in Uncle's direction. Uncle hadn't gone to sleep, but sleeping was definitely on his mind. He was standing beside the chair, his shirt off, suspenders unlatched, pants unzipped and hanging at half-mast.

"Uncle!" I cried, "What are you doing?"

Knowing that I could see well and was smart enough to figure out what he was doing, he responded sarcastically, "What do you think I'm doing? I'm getting ready for bed!" He pointed to the right where, if at home, his bed would have been.

I explained this amidst the polite, understanding chuckles of my friend and his family as I helped Uncle back into his shirt, scooped his pants up off the floor, hoisted them back to their proper place, and relatched his suspenders. He sheepishly complied with my every direction and later expressed the humiliation he had felt by remarking, "They must have thought I was crazy."

No, they didn't, Uncle. They have the utmost respect and admiration for you and think you are a wonderful and amazing person. They figure anybody else your age has been gone for years, and most of those who haven't wouldn't even attempt to do over several months what you do every day. You have every right in the world to get confused once in a while, so don't feel bad." Maybe it was my imagination, but I do believe my comments made him feel a whole lot better.

Uncle had another bout with confusion at the coast at a time when the whole family went over to spend the night. I had made reservations in an older, quaint, four-story hotel in Wheeler, perched in a beautiful setting overlooking Nehalem Bay. When I had stayed there a couple of times by myself, before Uncle had come aboard, I had gotten to know the very hospitable proprietor.

Our first meeting had been just by chance. I had spent the entire day calling on coastal dairymen and had several more calls to make when I ran out of appropriate business hours. Since it was already quite late, rather than make the two-plus hour trip home only to have to repeat it the next day, I decided to find a motel and spend the night. The chance was that I just happened to be near Gerta's Wheeler Inn, so I stopped and found a vacancy and rented a room. In the process of showing me the room, she invited me (after I'd dumped my things in the room) to come back to the office, which doubled for her apartment, for a nightcap and to visit with her evening's guest, the manager of the local bank, and herself. This I did, and in the months that followed I always had a place to cash checks. And every now and then, when in the area, I would run into Gerta and visit for a few minutes. It was during one of these visits that I learned of her concern and care for the elderly.

Gerta had several older boarders, a couple of them bedridden, to whom she gave better personal care than any hospital could afford. When Gerta heard about Uncle, she fell in love with him immediately, even before meeting him. So now I pulled the car around the backside of the hotel at a rather late hour. I went to Gerta's room, which is really two and doubles for the office. She appeared more than glad to see me and gave me the room keys. She told us to freshen up and come back down, all of us but especially Uncle, for some refreshments and a visit. We got there a bit after 10:00 pm and it was to be well after midnight before we headed back to our rooms. Judi, Cathi, Berniece and I had an extremely enjoyable time, but Uncle must have thought he had died and gone to heaven. Gerta hovered around him like a ministering angel. She poured glass after glass of wine for him, hung on his every word, asked him questions on everything from what it was like in his "old country, Norway (hers was Germany), to how he liked traveling with me. Moreover she did all of this without neglecting any of the rest of us. After about ninety minutes, the wine and the late hour got to Uncle and he dozed off. Gerta then gave Judi, the girls, and me her undivided attention, showing us every antique she had in her apartment and many other extremely interesting objects. For example, she shared with us the book that had been given to her brother, a WWII fighter pilot in Hitler's air force. Before we left, she had Cathi and Berniece pick out rings from a tray of them she had left over one of her previous businesses. The trinkets brought the girls months of pleasure.

Wearily but reluctantly, we finally excused ourselves, thanking Gerta profusely for a delightful evening. With Uncle in tow, we headed off to our rooms. As Judi and the girls were getting ready for bed in our room, I got Uncle into his, making sure he was comfortable, pointing out where everything was, and tucking him in before I left. Our room was right next to his, three floors up and on a hillside. I paused for a moment to take in the late night's beauty, from Wheeler's flickering street lights to the serenity of Nehalem Bay tucked between heavily forested hillsides and topped off by twinkling stars and a half moon. Once in the room, after a quick trip to the bathroom to "get rid of some water", as Uncle would say, I jumped into a bed already partially filled with Judi and was out like a light.

However, at approximately 2:30 am, I was awakened by our door being thrown open. Through bleary eyes I beheld Uncle wearing neither clothes nor glasses, cane in his hand hollering, "Jerry, Jerry!" I jumped up and ran to the door, seeing as I did the narrow walkway that went the full length of the building. Each floor had the same arrangement edged with only a low railing to keep anyone from plunging to the hard ground below. Uncle had wobbled back and forth, wearing only his jockey shorts and slippers, and miraculously hadn't fallen over the railing. This was material to make the most ardent skeptic a believer in guardian angels. I asked Uncle what he wanted, and he said he'd awakened and needed to go to the toilet but couldn't find it, so he went looking for me. I took him back to his room and showed him where his bathroom was, even helping him get tucked back into bed. I then told him in no uncertain terms that he must not leave the room until I came for him. Fortunately, he was able to make it through what was left of the night, and though he awakened early, I was very thankful for the help from above that preserved Uncle from a fatal fall. As I write, I can still see Uncle standing in my room's opened door, looking like a rather confused old ghost in white jockey shorts, hollering querulous "Jerrys" into the otherwise still night.

Due to the acquisition of his by now famous "pecker pouch", Uncle didn't have to go to the bathroom quite so often. This, however, didn't eliminate problems connected with this normal body function; the problems just changed form. For example, after he got pretty good at draining the thing all by himself, I often came out to the car and found a narrow yellow river up to forty feet long flowing out and away across the pavement. When I told him once that most people probably didn't appreciate a pouchful of urine dumped on their parking lots, he simply responded by saying, "Oh, a good rain will come along and wash it all away."

This problem wasn't too bad, though embarrassing at times; but occasions did arise when he'd forget where he was and, without opening the car door and draining the pouch outside, he'd simply open the valve and drain it on the floor. On one such occasion (and it happened more than once), I became understandably upset and demanded, "Uncle, why did you drain your pouch in the car instead of outside?" He violently denied having done so, and when after I suggested he touch the floorboard carpet, and his hand came up wet, he countered with, "The girls pissed on the floor and now you're trying to blame it on me!" When I traded in the Volare after 150,000 miles, they ended up having to rip up and replace all the carpets. Even that still didn't totally get rid of the smell.

The pouch was a godsend for taking care of the urine, but to my knowledge they've yet to come up with something as effective for the other end. Once again, we were up at the Medical School Hospital.

My brother, Charlie, was to spend several weeks up there, first for testicular cancer surgery, followed by extensive exploratory surgery and chemotherapy. I'd stop by frequently, either early in the morning or in the evening when I was coming home from making the rounds. This particular time was in the evening and again I had left Uncle in the car. While away, nature called. Uncle, who later insisted that he had waited as long as he could, left the car in the dark on a desperate search for a restroom. The Medical School, or University Hospital as it's called, is a maze of buildings built on a very precipitous hill overlooking downtown Portland. To maneuver all steps, slopes, turns, and obstacles of every description requires the vigor and reckless abandon of youth. So Uncle wandered from car to car, hoping somehow to make it to a building and a restroom. Finally, he gave up, leaned against a car, and did the only thing he'd found effective in the past – he began hollering, "Jerry, Jerry!" A couple of nurses, who were going from one part of the hospital to another, came along and, hearing Uncle's cries, asked if they could be of some help. He poured out the whole story, at least as he saw it.

"Jerry has left me here in the car and I've got to take a crap and I can't find a toilet."

With much care and a great deal of patience, and with one under each arm, they brought Uncle into the main building some fifty feet away and up a couple short flights of stairs to a restroom. I'd have loved to have seen and heard the conversation as those dear nurses backed Uncle up into one of the stalls, took off his jacket and sweater, loosened his suspenders, and situated his pouch before getting Uncle seated on the toilet. They managed very well apparently, but since they were already overdue at another place in the hospital, they called Security, explained the situation as best they could, and told them they must leave Uncle so Security had better send someone right away.

The security man found Uncle and assisted him through the paperwork stage and the redressing process. This, I know from lots of experience, requires patience and perseverance. All during this time, the security man tried to find out who Uncle was and where he belonged. He didn't make much headway in talking, so he pulled out Uncle's wallet and found, along with everything else, the names and phone numbers of his second cousins. With Uncle at his side, he made his way over to a phone, pulled up a chair for Uncle, and dialed Ruth and Esther. All he got was a busy signal, so he dialed the operator saying he had an emergency and needed her to break in on the conversation. I was later informed by Ruth that she was talking to a relative who was telling her about a recent family member's death when their conversation was interrupted. She took it all in good stride, informing the security man that Uncle was the charge of one Gary Gorsuch who must be visiting his brother, Charles, who was presently a patient in the University Hospital. With that information, the guard was able to find out what floor Brother Charles was on and have a nurse check to see if I was with him.

Sure enough, there I was and within a few minutes I was where they told me I could collect Uncle. When I arrived, Uncle was seated in a comfortable chair, coated and capped, with both hands resting on the cane between his legs. He was deep into a conversation with the fully-uniformed security officer who squatted beside Uncle, totally captivated by him. I quickly came over and almost had to produce I.D.

before the guard would relinquish what now had become "his" charge. He then assured me Uncle was OK and told me about having to look into his wallet, being careful to say that he'd found five dollars in it which I might want to verify was still in there. He then told of making the calls, getting Ruth by having the operator break into her conversation, and the events with the nurses that led up to his involvement. I thanked him and went to help Uncle up to take him back to the car and home. Even though I assured the guard that I could manage myself, he went with me, supporting Uncle and reassuring him each step of the way. When we parted, I almost expected a tear or two from the guard. In an amazingly short period of time, Uncle had evidently endeared himself to another heart.

Another morning when I stopped by to visit my brother in the hospital, Uncle's confusion got him into some hot water. After carefully explaining to Uncle where I'd be and assuring him I'd only be gone for about thirty minutes, I left the car. Sometime during my absence, because with Uncle time really meant very little, he got restless, opened the car door, and went for a walk. With his poor eyesight confused by the thousands of cars, Uncle got lost almost immediately. He couldn't have been far from our car when he found another which looked similar; he tried the door, it opened, so he climbed in. Minutes later, a young mother with a babe in arms and a child in tow came out from the hospital to get into her car and head on home. It wasn't to be that easy. Whom should she find firmly fixed into the front passenger seat of her car? You guessed it – Uncle! I'm sure she tried pleasantly, after getting over her initial shock, to talk Uncle into leaving peaceable, but he wouldn't budge.

"This is my car," cried the distracted mother.

"No, it's not!" was Uncle's stubborn reply, with an "Are you crazy?! thrown in for good measure.

Apparently she noticed our Volare close by, put two and two together, and with the proper amount of encouragement and her help, got Uncle back where he belonged. When I came out, Uncle was in his regular spot and anxious to tell me all the details of how he got lost and ended up in the wrong car. His precision about all the details and the number of his "Boy, oh boy's", "Are you crazy's", and his trenchant observation that "She was hopping mad," convince me that the incident happened as or close to that I've described. In fact, the more I think about it, I'm probably only telling a small part of all that really happened. We need someone like Paul Harvey to bump into the woman sometime in the future and tell "the rest of the story."

Uncle went with Judi and me to a three-day, two-night Washington Dairyman's State Convention in Kelso, Washington. The three of us shared a romantic honeymoon room. The only problem turned out to be little or no loving and even less sleep.

Uncle could never sleep very well in strange surroundings. That, along with the fact that I hate to be away from my family, kept my overnight trips to the bare minimum. At night he'd moan and groan, complain, his pouch would leak, and he'd get up and wander around the room at all hours. As if these disturbances weren't bad enough, I could expect several times during the night to have Uncle break forth in full voice, "Jerry, Jerry, Jerry!" and then ask me to check and see if his glasses were still on the table or night stand, what time we'd be getting up, or answer some other question that really (at least to my way of thinking) was not important enough to rouse me from my sleep. Unfortunately, this trip was no exception to the pattern. Fortunately for Judi she can sleep through almost anything and do so in grand style.

The first day we set up our display table in one of the main hallways in the Kelso Thunderbird, the motor inn where the convention was to be held as well as where we were staying. I found an overstuffed chair near our table for Uncle in plain view of where I'd be spending most of my time. Uncle used this opportunity to catch up on all the sleep we'd lost the night before, at least until they opened up the dairy bar conveniently positioned right across from his chair. I got him started by asking him if he'd like some cheese and crackers, so I guess I'm the one to blame for the problem that later would develop. "Why sure," said Uncle, and I brought him a nice handful, which in nothing flat he gobbled down and asked for more. I waited on him several times but soon got busy meeting people and discussing our products, pretty much leaving uncle to fend for himself. I later learned that he had recruited a couple of women who were helping serve. They beat a trail back and forth with paper plate after plate of cheese and crackers. Uncle must have put away three or four pounds of cheese during the days of that convention. I was initially pleased because he really enjoyed it and, since he didn't get sick, all those munchies gave him a pleasant way to spend what otherwise could have been long, boring hours.

The problem all this cheese caused wasn't to surface for a couple days after the convention when we discovered that the large quantity he consumed had plugged up his system. It had been several days since his last bowel movement. We were out on the road going from

146

dairy to dairy when finally the pressure reached an uncomfortable level and Uncle asked me to stop and purchase some sort of laxative. I bought him a bottle of Phillips Milk of Magnesia. I unscrewed the cap, and gave Uncle a little sip, capped it back, and slid the bottle underneath the seat. Out of sight, out of mind.

A few more miles down the road, I stopped to visit another dairyman, a typical call to build toward that day when I could sign him up for a major purchase. Then I returned to the car, took one look at Uncle, and said to myself, "I knew it was bound to happen! Uncle has finally gone off his rocker." I took a closer look and saw that the white around his lips didn't after all indicate frothing at the mouth. There, lying beside him, was the nearly-empty bottle of Phillips. Filled with awful visions of the certain future, I broke all speed limits.

We almost made it home before the dam gave way. I was pulling into the driveway when Uncle cried, "I can't hold it any longer!" With those ominous words came a hiss and lots of rumbling and a wall of stench that would make a waste disposal plant smell like a perfume factory.

I pulled the Volare to a stop, went around the car, and helped Uncle up from his formerly tan-colored seat which was now a sludgy, odiferous brown. I hustled Uncle into the house and straight into the bathroom. As I began peeling off the layers of clothing, I found that he'd filled his shorts, pants, and even his boots. I sat him on the toilet and he proceeded to fill up a couple of flushes' worth before finally it stopped coming. In the process, Uncle must have dropped ten or fifteen pounds. It was only after a long, hot shower and several re-washings that Uncle and his clothes were fit to be admitted into human company.

The results of Uncle's Kelso cheese binge, with its subsequent eruption problem, remind me of another tale or two from the Kelso convention that shouldn't be left untold. For example, we lost Uncle on the day we were to leave. He's a person of many extremes who seldom can be found on middle ground on any issue. For example, he's either still as death or constantly poking, fidgeting, or moving about.

At other meetings, it wasn't uncommon to have a dairyman come up to me and say, "Gary, I just passed Uncle headed South down the far hallway hollering, 'Jerry, Jerry!' You'd better go after him." I'd always find him never once worse for the wear.

This time, after getting everything packed and saying our last goodbyes, we went to claim Uncle from that comfortable chair we'd left him in just minutes before. When we arrived, Uncle was gone. We frantically looked about, even notifying the Inn's staff, who searched each and every hallway with their elaborate closed-circuit camera system, sending other staff members to search areas where this was impossible. Still no Uncle. Finally, just before heading outside to comb the parking lot and adjoining properties, I went to the area where our room had been. I stopped at the room and knocked, and a middle aged man cautiously poked his head out of the partially-opened door. He acted as if he'd been bothered earlier, and sure enough Uncle had been by claiming that this was his room. The guy had held his ground, not giving an inch, and finally, Uncle gave up in disgust and shuffled off down the hallway. I went down the direction the man had pointed and one more turn and thirty or forty feet further, there was Uncle, seated in a little alcove, which explained why he couldn't be seen by the scanning system. He, content as can be, was visiting with one of the maids.

That's not to say that there weren't some close calls. Once in the scenic Columbia River Gorge town of The Dalles, on the way home from the Yakima Valley, I stopped at a phone booth to make a call. I didn't awaken Uncle, figuring I'd quickly take care of my business and continue on home. I got busy on the phone. With Uncle just a few feet behind me, seated safely in the car nosed up against the phone booth, I chatted away. Several minutes later, as the conversation began to wind down, I glanced at the road that ran beside the phone booth on toward the river. About a hundred and fifty feet down the road, I noticed the back side of a very interesting old man. He was hobbling along, cane in hand and flat cap on his head, looking just like Uncle. He had almost reached the point where the road took a hard left and ran parallel to the river. "My, my!" I said to myself. "Two of them in the world!" And I casually turned to get a glimpse of Uncle. The door was open and he was gone! The coincidence clicked. The stranger who looked so much like Uncle was Uncle.

I hung up the phone with some incoherent remark about Uncle and the river, jumped into the car, and sped down the road. In the time it took me to get into the car, turn it around and start off, Uncle had already rounded the corner and vanished from sight. I turned left, following the road, and there came upon a modest trailer and a scene that should be immortalized on canvas. Uncle stood in the yard right in front of the trailer house door, shaking his cane in disgust at an Indian woman who had one arm wrapped completely around a small dog and the other free, her hand resting on the door knob. Uncle, in his heavy Norwegian accent, with his upper denture slipping down and rattling every few words, was asking the woman if she knew where his bed was. I collected Uncle and in all the excitement offered little explanation to the puzzled Indian woman, who appeared to be clutching her dog even tighter as we turned to leave. The best explanation I could get out of Uncle was that he'd awakened and, thinking we were home, had gotten out of the car to go into the house and his bed. He thanked me profusely for his rescue, saying, "Goodness knows what might have happened if you, Jerry, hadn't come along." I was just thankful that the ending was so sweet and that in about two hours we'd be home where I'd see to it personally that, after dinner, Uncle found his bed.

Getting out of the car, whether out of curiosity or confusion, was a common practice of Uncle's. At a Gladstone, Oregon, Burgerville restaurant he was to do it again. I was involved with estimating the cost-effectiveness of a refrigeration/heat-recovery system. Used on dairies for years, it had a similar application for many other businesses. Any operation that used lots of hot water and had large refrigeration requirements was a candidate, so restaurants were a natural. I must have been inside for close to an hour, though I had been able to check on Uncle by looking through a window several times, and he appeared to be resting nicely. All at once, a frantic pounding sounded at the back door and the manager let in a frightened young lady who was just arriving for her work shift. She blurted out her story – an old man in the parking lot was yelling at her.

I knew what had happened. Uncle had gotten tired of waiting

again and climbed out of the car, not knowing where he was or why and was calling for me. About this time, the young lady had showed up, parked her car, and began walking the few feet to the restaurant. To get there, she had to walk past Uncle. She'd probably never seen anybody as old as Uncle outside of a hospital or a rest home, and the fact that he had a heavy Norwegian accent, I'm sure, didn't help matters any. He had called to her, apparently wanting her to find me or to help him back into the car. Naturally, she thought that she was being propositioned by the original "dirty old man." I assured her that he was completely harmless, and after I was able to calm her down, I went out and folded Uncle safely back into the car, where he was content to remain until I completed the testing.

On another day, not many miles away, I was doing some similar work at the Wilsonville Vip's Restaurant and left Uncle sleeping in the car. He awoke and as before, thinking he was home, got out of the car and walked the few feet to the almost adjoining motel. He tried a locked room door. About that time I came out for one of my regular checks and found Uncle banging on a motel room door with his cane hollering, "Jerry, Jerry!" I hustled over and gently told Uncle that this wasn't our home and I would help him back into the car. "It's not?" he said. "Well, I do declare." And then he calmly climbed back into his front passenger seat and soon was again fast asleep.

One of my daughters always has had more important things to do than to clean her room. In fact, she has a poster thumb-tacked onto her door which reads, "A clean room is a sure sign of a sick mind." One morning, Uncle rolled out of bed several hours early and stumbled into her room. Before leaving, he succeeded in waking Cathi, conducted a distorted conversation, turned around, left her room, and climbed back into his bed. The next morning, he told us that he had had the strangest dream. He'd been sleeping on the West Burnside sidewalk, Portland skid row, and rolled off into the gutter. He'd picked himself up, dusted off his clothing, and walked into the first doorway he came to. "The shop", he said disgustedly, "was filled with yunk. There was yunk all over the place. I asked who owned the shop and someone said, 'This is Cathi's shop.' Well, I don't know who this Cathi was, but that was the worst mess I'd ever laid my eyes on."

"Out of the mouth of babes" is a common expression to describe frank, honest, appraisals or evaluations. Uncle was no babe, but the same kind of honesty totally permeated his being. Cathi hasn't changed that much in how she cares for her room, but I'll bet many times as she views the "yunk all over the place", the memories of the strange, early-morning visitation come back to her.

Three blankets were enough to keep Uncle warm as long as one of them, the closest to him, was electric. The problem was that uncle's electric blanket didn't stay that way for long. Whenever Uncle awoke, he was constantly probing, poking, and feeling. He'd stay in bed usually (but not always, alas) until daylight or when I got up. God only knows how much of his time in bed was spent awake or asleep. One of the things that he'd play with during his awake time was the electric blanket. More than once he'd feel along and find a lump where some of the wires came together and then, thinking it was some type of imperfection, he'd pull out his folding knife, the one with the five-inch blade, and cut the lump out. After the destruction of two electric blankets and the shredding of a couple of his pecker pouches, I finally lost his knife for him. It's right across from where his cane got lost, in a top left-hand drawer. I use it myself every once in a while for carving.

Another time Uncle must have dreamed someone broke into our house for he called me downstairs very early, telling me all about the burglar who broke in and how he had subdued him. Then, pointing to the empty chair, he proudly proclaimed, "He's all tied up over there." I was thankful then that his knife was "lost!" No telling what kind of damage to himself or someone or something he could have done.

This next anecdote raises a speculation that Uncle wasn't confused after all but rather, with his many unique abilities, he could have been seeing into the future. I say this because just a few weeks after Uncle's death, a burglar actually struck. It was for that very reason I had gotten Boris, our 175-pound black Great Dane. Just two weeks earlier, Judi had bought me (for Boris, on our anniversary!) a three-inch wide black studded collar bristling with two rows of one and a half-inch stainless-steel spikes. It created just the right effect. Even people whom we knew well and who understood that our new canine was really a sheep in wolf's clothing wouldn't get out of their cars. They now waited until one of us came out to escort them into the house. Therefore, I was as confident as can be that no burglar in his right mind would attempt to ply his trade among our possessions. With big, black, beautiful Boris on the job, we had nothing to worry about.

A couple of weeks after Boris had been outfitted with the new collar, I came home after a long day on the road. Home always looks good and that day was no exception. I drove up the 150-foot driveway under the precipitous fir tree, which always reminded me of Uncle's words of warning. Maybe I'd better do something about that tree. I pulled to a stop just to the left of the corner deck-post and turned off the motor. Boris lumbered out to greet me, his tail and whole rear end wagging furiously. Something did not look quite right, but in my eagerness to get into the house and all the love the three women in my life shower continuously upon me, I dismissed the thought. I climbed out of the car, but before I could advance more than a few feet, both Cathi and Berniece dashed out of the house yelling that we'd been robbed. Closer examination revealed that items ranging from Judi's hand painted Portuguese plates and platters to an old cream separator had disappeared. Jewelry, a portable cassette stereo, the antique clock, mirror, and figurines, plus a large white ceramic Great Dane statue that we'd picked up long before Boris arrived on the scene.

As if this weren't painful enough, when I went outside to check for tire tracks, footprints, or other tell-tale signs, Boris padded out to greet me again from his newly-completed A-frame doghouse. I'd cut down a cedar tree and split up a number of shakes and put a twenty-year roof on his house, which meant that his protection from the elements was in better shape than our own. I gave him a grim pat on the head and then moved my hand idly across the top of his head and down his neck. And I figured out what didn't look quite right – Boris' collar was gone! The burglars must have had trouble leaving the scene of their crime, but not from Boris. They surely had to be laughing so hard that they were barely able to control their vehicle as they wound their way back down our driveway. Two of the items they probably didn't even try to fence were the big white dog and Boris' black studded and spiked collar. These mementos must have a prominent place in their plush penthouse. There sits a tangible reminder of success – the big white plaster Great Dane with its neck adorned by the three-inch, $50 spiked collar.

While getting special, intense, one-day sales training in Seattle from a firm called Organizational Developers, I'd brought Uncle along for lack of a better way to take care of him. The company was owned and operated by a former university professor, Bob McDonald, and his young wife, Skip. Skip had an adorable preschool child who was very precocious. When I told Bob that "where Jerry went, Uncle went" he sent me back out to the car to get him and said he'd put Skip's daughter in charge of keeping an eye on him. So I brought Uncle into the house. Once inside, he was made comfortable in a living room overstuffed chair, given a cup of coffee, and after explaining that I'd be downstairs going through some training, I went to their daylight basement where the office and training facilities were located. The arrangement seemed superb. Every hour or so I'd take a break and run up to double-check on Uncle.

But about two-thirds the way through the morning, the youngster came down and said that Uncle was moving around quite a bit and had started using some mean words. I excused myself and quickly went up and did what I could to settle Uncle back down. He seemed to understand when I re-explained what was going on and soon settled right down. However, what seems to be true often isn't; Uncle hadn't understood a word I'd said. He didn't know where he was, why he'd been left sitting in a strange living room doing nothing, and the longer he sat like this, the madder he got. Finally, about thirty minutes before we'd have stopped for lunch, Uncle blew up. The youngster, who'd really done a flawless job, rushed into the training area crying, "The old man is very angry! You'd better come quick!! I bolted from my seat and rushed to the stairs. That's as far as I got. Uncle was already half the way down them. The second he saw me he shrieked all sorts of accusations, calling me everything horrible he could think of. He then went into a wanting-to-kill-me rage, shaking his cane, threatening all sorts of ways he'd like to make my death happen. Bob was right behind me, totally speechless.

After what seemed like many minutes Bob said, "Let's go ahead and break for lunch and we'll finish up this afternoon. He then told me where the nearest restaurant was, suggesting that maybe after Uncle had some food he'd settle down. Uncle was still shouting and shaking his cane as I carefully assisted him back up the stairs and out to the car. I had to do a lot of talking once we got to the restaurant even to get Uncle to go in. Once inside, I ordered one of his favorites, chili and corn bread, with lots of coffee to wash the whole works down. At first, he refused to eat, but finally, with just a bit more grumbling, the sight and aroma of the food proved to be too much to resist and he slowly began to eat. After about the third tentative spoonful of chili, he settled into his normal lustful slurping and chomping and before my very eyes reverted back to his normal, passive (if not fully pleasant at least peaceful) self. We finished lunch without further incident, I got Uncle out to the car, and we drove back to the McDonalds's.

Bob must have been watching for us. No sooner had I pulled into the driveway than he was out to ask how things were going. I said, "He's calmed down now and should do just fine sitting and sleeping in the car." I explained that after eating, he usually dozes off, and what better place than in the familiar surrounds of his seat in the Volare. Bob agreed but had one suggestion that proved to be the clincher for an uneventful Uncle afternoon.

"I'll get him a glass of wine." And what a glass it was. Bob brought out a large water glass brimming with an excellent vintage of white wine. Before we left the car to resume downstairs, Uncle had drunk two-thirds of it and responded with a hearty, "Boy, oh boy, is that good!" He placed the glass with what was left in the plastic cup holder that hung to his right and settled back for what was to be one of the longest naps he'd taken in years. Though I checked on him four or five times during the next several hours, I really didn't need to. Uncle even slept most of the three and a half hour ride home that evening. From that time on, I was very careful not to put Uncle into such an uncomfortably unfamiliar environment. Though at the time his behavior was extremely trying, even then I admired his spunk and spirit.

On one of my visits to Elenbaas' home office in Lynden near Bellingham, Washington, I stayed with my sister, Margaret, and my niece, Suzanne, and nephew, John. Just before we left to head back down to Portland, we got together with my oldest brother, Harvey, at a restaurant for a parting breakfast. Uncle was in good form and when he finally figured out who everyone was, including me, he reveled in reliving some of his past experiences with us. First he spoke of the time Harvey had backed me up into a corner with a pitchfork in his hand, saying "This is the way we spear the natives in India." This incident arose from the WWII influence of our Uncle Johnny, who didn't actually spear natives but did tell us about some of the primitive people there. Our wild imaginations took it from there. Well, about that time, as Uncle tells the story, he came along and saved the day, at least for me.

"Oh, no, you don't," he said, as he jerked the pitchfork out of Harvey's hands. "Off Harv went," says Uncle, "crying 'Momma, Momma!' Then your mother tied into me, saying I was picking on the kids. Boy, oh boy. But Jerry had a way to get even. He'd sneak up behind Harvey and grab him around the neck so he couldn't move and bite him on the ear lobe. He wouldn't draw blood, but boy, oh boy, how'd Harvey squeal."

Uncle told a story or two more and then with eyes brimming, said, "It's been so nice that all you people have thrown this party for me." During most of the meal, Uncle was so grateful for the "party" thrown in his honor that his emotions gained the upper hand and he just sat there softly sobbing. We were many miles down the road before all the tears finished drying up. Later, in referring to that experience, he would say, "And a good time was had by all."

On one of our trips, Uncle and I stayed overnight with my youngest sister, Miriam, her husband, John, and their two children, Andrew and Audrey Anna. Unfortunately, as was almost always the case, Uncle was uncomfortable at not being in his own bed. He stated in no uncertain terms that he wanted to sleep in his own bed in Sherwood. Having slept all the way up, he must have figured we couldn't be any more than a few minutes away from home. When I explained that Sherwood was almost four hours away, he blurted out right in front of Miriam and the small children, "B-B-B-Bull Shit!" Miriam, who'd never heard a cross or crude word from Uncle, went into shock for a full fifteen seconds and then began laughing uncontrollably. Andrew and Audrey Anna, who never hear such language in their home, were also caught off guard, but they soon recovered to accuse in unison, "Mommy! Uncle said a naughty word."

One last account of confusion (or at least I hope it was) involved but wasn't directly Uncle's. It was during the last two weeks of Uncle's life. He was in the King City Care Center unable to walk and slipping fast. I'd stop by usually every day, sometimes twice, and often after a long day on the road. This particular time, I had to search quite a while before finding Uncle. He was sitting in his wheelchair, strapped in so he wouldn't fall out, in one of the several television rooms. There were two other people in the room, neither of whom was paying any attention to the blaring television. Even though he wasn't responding, I gave him a run-down of the day's events, conveying greetings from the many dairymen who truly missed not seeing him. I sat facing him, and every once in a while he'd give my hand a hearty squeeze.

As I talked, an elderly woman, whom I assumed was in the later stages of senility, motored up in her wheelchair kind of crab style, with her legs doing all the work, continually muttering to herself. She gradually worked herself up to within a few feet of me, looked me right in the eye, and said as clear and plain as it could be said by anyone, "You should be ashamed of yourself." She then hesitated and added, "You know what I mean." Then she went back to her incoherent babbling and crab-walked over to a far corner of the room. I got up, gave Uncle a quick squeeze, told him I'd see him the next day, and slithered towards the hall. I felt a strange guiltiness. Then the words of my mother echoed in my mind, "Uncle will never go to a rest home as long as I have anything to say about it." She had died four years earlier and no longer had any say . . . I glanced one final time at the woman in the corner and left.

15

MANY HANDS MAKE LIGHT WORK . . . ?

U ncle is progressing quite well. By that, I mean the infection has been brought under control and the swelling and inflammation have been reduced considerably. Uncle's been in the hospital for over a week now, but his overall health, apart from the infection, has not improved. If anything, it's deteriorated a bit more. He still refuses to walk, isn't eating very well, continues to be anemic, and has an abdominal thrombosis. Dr. Morita has mentioned that he's considering a couple pints of blood after the infection is cleared up.

I've held out as long as I can and told the doctor that unless Uncle can walk and eat, he'd not be in any condition to ride the range with me. Sad, since there's usually nobody at home during the day, some other arrangements would have to be made. I know Dr. Morita has admired the way our family has been willing and somehow able to make the adjustments and sacrifices to care for Uncle. I feel he's sad that our mostly happy compromise may now have to come to an end. He reassures me that he'll do his best and leans down to speak full-voiced into Uncle's ear, trying to encourage him to make the extra effort to walk and eat. If Uncle doesn't respond, it won't be due to inferior care! All the care-givers I've witnessed around Uncle have gone the extra mile and then some to give above and beyond the call of duty. I suppose I should know at least as well as anyone the qualities within Uncle that most of the time made it a pleasure to serve him. The helping went both ways, but where Uncle was involved, the outcome wasn't always predictable.

Like the time I stopped to mow Uncle's lawn. Before finishing, I took a breather and began visiting with Nels across the street. He was amazed how fit Uncle was, especially since Uncle was thirty-five years his senior. "Quite a guy," was my reply, and Nels was quick to agree.

"Been a real good neighbor," Nels said. "When I've ever asked him for a helping hand, Charlie has always come through, sometimes a little too well. Take the time I asked him to watch my house a couple years back when we went to California. Charlie took the job too seriously! He finally realized he couldn't walk around the house twenty-four hours a day, and he was fearful that while he slept or was away, he'd miss seeing someone prying open a window. He solved the problem in a hurry; he nailed the windows shut through the wooden sashes with sixteen-penny nails. Every damn window." I had trouble finishing the lawn after that account, I was laughing so hard. Nel's remark on Uncle's physical condition was even further heightened when I heard that Nels died a year and a half or so before Uncle.

One way Uncle's helping hands endeared him forever to us Gorsuch children was what he did for our mother. Uncle's first wife was my mother's aunt, her mother's sister, Gertrude. In the thirties, after Gertrude and Uncle had been married for something over ten years, she said to Uncle, "Say, Charlie, what are you going to do with all this money you've been saving up?"

"Oh," said Uncle, "I thought maybe you and me would go over to the Mediterranean and cruise around on one of those big ships and see what the natives are like over there."

"I've got a better idea," said Gertrude. "I've got a couple of nieces on the plains of North Dakota, and I'd like to educate them."

Without so much as a pause to think it over to ask how much money it would take, he responded, "OK." Not many days later, they set off from Portland in their new Chevrolet accompanied by eight spare tires, all of which had to be used before they even got through Montana. Once in North Dakota, and after a several-week visit, my ready and willing mother and aunt, with much excitement and anticipation, left with Uncle Charlie and Aunt Gertrude, who brought them back to Portland where they finished high school and then went on to Portland State College. They then transferred up to Pacific Lutheran in Tacoma, where my aunt graduated, while my Mother went over to Washington State to graduate with a teaching certificate in home economics.

Their education served our family, which included seven children, well in the years that followed. Mother taught school for over thirty years to ease the financial load, while at the same time being a wife and mother. The many fond memories and words of appreciation I've heard from both my mother and aunt for the loving generosity, care, and concern of Aunt Gertrude and Uncle Charlie have been and will continue to be a fitting memorial and example to us Gorsuch's and our cousins.

Before Uncle moved in with us, as some of the previous tales have mentioned, I'd often stop by his home and help him with various projects and chores. Sometimes he'd give me a dollar or two, if he happened to think of it, depending on how much he felt my aid was worth. Once, he was so impressed with what I'd done that he marched me down into the basement and insisted that I take all his tools.

"I don't have any use for them," he said dramatically. "Take them all."

I declined, but he became so insistent that I finally loaded up a couple small fruit boxes, being careful to leave him an assortment of hammers, pliers, screwdrivers, and saws so that he'd have the basics if needed. I thanked him profusely and headed home. The very next day the phone rang. It would continue to ring for the next few weeks as Uncle started asking that I return this, then that, until he got back almost every tool I'd taken, plus a few of my own. Aw, well, it's the thought that counts, and with Uncle, he was always thinking.

A few months before Uncle came to live permanently with us, we had him out to Sherwood for Thanksgiving Day for the traditional dinner. We felt Uncle was a very important part of that special day. I went into Portland to pick him up, and at the same time, I picked up Ruth and Esther. Lots of food and plenty of good conversation provided a truly delightful time for all. By the time the festivities began to break up, it was starting to get dark. Judi, the girls and I, along with Uncle, Ruth and Esther piled into the car to take everyone home. We dropped Ruth and Esther off first, and once we were sure they were safely inside, took Uncle to his Failing Street home. As we neared Uncle's house, we saw a number of people gathered on Uncle's porch. We soon found out that Uncle had taken no chance on missing out on a delicious Thanksgiving turkey dinner. One of the neighbors had offered the evening before to come by with a plate loaded with turkey and all the trimmings and Uncle had graciously accepted. The problem was that he failed to mention that he'd been invited out to Sherwood for the day.

The neighbor had come in the late afternoon with Uncle's promised plate and of course got no response. He rang the doorbell, banged on the door, and called at each and every window. Nothing worked. Finally, he went home and called the police, positive that something awful had happened to Uncle and that he was lying helpless in the basement, on the stairs, or in the bedroom. Well, the police came and they were now, along with many other neighbors, gathered on and around Uncle's porch. As we pulled up, the police were trying to pick Uncle's front door lock.

I apologized to the officers and the neighbors, who thankfully seemed understanding enough. Finally, after we answered several questions, the police left and crowd disappeared. Uncle later called to chuckle about the event wondering if he'd gotten in on all that had happened. In other words, he wondered if he'd missed something in the excitement of the moment that I hadn't. To him, it had been truly an event to savor.

At Sunnyside, in the beautiful Yakima Valley, right in the middle of a conversation with a dairyman who was soon to need a milk tank, Uncle gave me his usual three blasts on the car's horn. Before I could find a convenient place in our conversation to excuse myself, Uncle thumped out another three blasts. I interrupted the dairyman in mid-sentence, saying that I needed to check on my 98-year-old Uncle. When I got to the car, Uncle said, Get me to a crap can quick!" I scooted him out of the car and shouted over to the dairyman, asking him if he had a restroom in the milk house. "No," he replied. "Bring him up to the house."

As is often the case, the house was quite a ways from the farm building where we were parked. I was dreadfully aware that getting in and out of the car caused a strain, so we followed the dairyman already heading out across to the house. With Uncle leaning on my arm, I aimed for the house some 300 feet away. About half way there, Uncle pulled me to a stop, grimaced in what seemed pain, squeezed his legs and buttocks together, and moaned, "It's coming, and I don't think I can stop it." We stood there as he struggled, and then when it appeared he'd done all he could, we proceeded the rest of the way and into the house and the closest bathroom. I got Uncle's coat, sweater, one of his two shirts, suspenders, pants, and then his lumpy jockey shorts down.

Yes, Uncle had been right – he hadn't been able to hold it. Resigned, I sat him down on the toilet, giving him the opportunity to evacuate anything that still remained in his bowel. There wasn't much of anything left. I then cleaned him up as best I could, using what seemed like half a roll of toilet paper. It took several flushes to get the whole mess down. Finally, as Uncle was to say more than once during his "Jerry"-assisted trips to the "the crap can", "Oh, that's good enough; the rest will dry." Ignoring that blithe comment, I completed the paperwork to my standards.

Then, with Uncle still seated, I pulled out my little Swiss Army knife that had a small pair of scissors and I cut his jockey shorts off him one leg at a time. That way, I didn't have to jerk Uncle's boots and pants off to get the "loaded" shorts out of the way. I didn't figure on keeping the shorts, so my concern was to get them off the quickest, easiest, and cleanest way possible. Once off, my next problem was disposing of them. They couldn't be flushed down the toilet, though I did get rid of some of their contents that way, but glancing around, I spotted a trash can. I carefully folded up Uncle's shorts and stuffed them deep into the trash. I hoped someone would be emptying the thing soon. After I got Uncle dressed, I bid my customer good day with many thank-yous, and we made our escape.

Over two hundred miles from Sunnyside, in a town just a few miles southeast of Portland, Uncle once again got into a similar situation, though through no fault of his own. I had stopped to check out a heat recovery system which we installed in Jim Goldt's J's Family Restaurant in Clackamas, Oregon. I ended up meeting and having a cup of coffee there with an old friend, a salesman from my A-1 Electric days whom I hadn't seen for years. We became so absorbed in the conversation that I didn't keep a very close eye on Uncle. After about forty-five minutes, we got up to leave. As we walked up to the cashier, I overheard her talking to the police.

"Yes," she said, "Apparently someone has just abandoned an old man in our parking lot . . . "

Horrified, I interrupted her before she could say anything more. "Hey, I think you're talking about the person I'm in charge of. I'm on my way out right now to check on him."

She gave me a scum-of-the-earth look and said, "You mean you've been sitting over there," and she looked in the direction we just came from, "and didn't see or hear any of the commotion going on over your charge? While you were sitting enjoying your coffee, he was out in the parking lot leaning on the car horn. He finally got the attention of a woman who was on her way into the restaurant. She went over to the car, but she wasn't able to understand him very well, so she came in here and asked if anyone knew what a "crap can" was. A gentleman nearby said it was a toilet and offered to go out and see if he could assist the old man. He went out and took your charge to the restroom in here and then took him back out to the car."

I apologized for the inconvenience I'd caused, thanked her for her concern and help, and paid my bill – all to the tune of her continual attitude of disdain and disgust. Then I slinked out to check on Uncle. By that time, Uncle was sleeping soundly, perfectly content, appearing exactly as I'd left him some fifty minutes earlier. Being concerned that the young cashier didn't have all the facts, though granted I'd been neglectful, I got one of our newsletters with an article about Uncle and me and went back into the restaurant and gave it to her. She took it, though I'm not sure she'd read it. I'd probably have felt the same way under similar circumstances. I wished I could have thanked our unsung hero, but the reward for him must have been the pleasure of being able to assist a fellow man in need. (I'm sure that sometime in the future, someone, somewhere, will have the privilege of repaying my debt.)

16

IF YOU WANT MY ADVICE . . . OR EVEN IF YOU DON'T

D r. Morita has given Uncle the units of blood he'd talked about and the urinary tract infection totally cleared up. The blood didn't make any contribution to improving Uncle's mobility or overall condition, however. He still didn't want to eat and refused, in spite of considerable prodding, to get up and move about. He preferred just lying in bed and had almost to be forced into getting up even to sit in his bed-side chair. About the only positive event during those last few days in the hospital was his one request that the nurses take him for a ride in one of their cars. Unfortunately, such an outing was impossible at the time, and he never asked again.

An abdominal aneurysm developed, and apparently a slight stroke caused a throat paralysis making it difficult for Uncle to swallow. Dr. Morita stretched to the limit the time Uncle could remain in the hospital, but finally the decision had to be made to discharge him to a Care Center. The day and the hour were set for his move, and I planned to hustle back from a scheduled trip to Tillamook. As it turned out, the hospital's transportation service moved him to the King City Care Center before I was able to get back. When I called the hospital to tell them that I'd be a few minutes late, they told me that

169

he'd already been transferred. The move, however, went very smoothly without me, handled by people who did this sort of thing every day.

So when I came into town, I went directly to the Care Center where I spent about an hour filling out forms and signing papers after first checking on Uncle. Upon completing all the admitting procedures, I introduced myself to the Care Center's administrator, Mr. Wall. He was an extremely pleasant person who discussed his background and the significant place older family members played in his life. It was easy for me to see how he'd ended up in this profession, and I was able to empathize with much that he talked about. Having counseled many people in similar situations to mine, he was able to give me quite a bit of direction in dealing with this stage of Uncle's condition.

Direction or advice was something Uncle dispensed freely and which definitely should be included in this book. Some of it wasn't worth much, but a lot of it was priceless.

I don't care what the subject, Uncle had something to say about it. During the Iranian captivity of 1980 through January, 1981, news reporters provided continual updates. Since we kept the radio on most of the time, Uncle got in on quite a bit of the information as soon as it became available. Every time he heard hostage news, he'd recount how he'd handle the situations, if he had anything to say about it. He'd get all worked up, clench his teeth, and in a fierce, forceful, higher-than-normal pitch declare, "I would give those Iranians an ultimatum. And if they didn't release the hostages, I'd drop an atomic bomb and blow them off the face of the earth. There are some people you just can't reason with."

He had similar sentiments for three fellows who'd killed a number of helpless people over a several-month-period. The last victim was a 14-year-old neighbor girl who was nabbed in broad daylight off one of our country roads, abused by all three, and then violently murdered. This tragedy struck very close to us, since the girl had been in our home many times and my youngest daughter, Berniece, had spent the entire day with the girl and her family the day before she was killed. The local uproar that followed produced a ten-thousand-dollar reward that led to the murderers' capture and later, a conviction. Uncle's advice was to take them downtown and hang them by their necks from telephone poles, leaving their bodies there several days so people could see what becomes of those who commit such acts. Then "we wouldn't have as many problems with that sort of thing."

Uncle's advice was available in family matters, too. In February of '81, the main breaker in our electrical panel had to be replaced. Uncle, who didn't want to miss a single thing, had to be informed down to the last detail what had happened and how I was going to fix it. Though very handy himself, if he didn't know how to fix or repair an item, then the only hope was to hire a professional. In this case it was a professional electrician. After pulling the meter which completely cut off the power to the house, filled with the determination that Uncle's words gave me ("You can't fix it. You'll electrocute yourself. Get a professional."), I replaced the breaker. When I told Uncle and showed him that I'd done it, he came forth with an unbelieving and awed, "Ya?" and wouldn't even give me the satisfaction of any additional praise or comment.

Once near Ridgefield, Washington, I stopped at a service station grocery store to get directions. Uncle stayed in the car, which I left running with the transmission in park. Before I could open my mouth to ask directions, the lady calmly inquired, "Was that your car that just crashed into the fence behind the store?"

"No," I said turning, "My car is right over . . . "It was gone!

I burst out the door not knowing what kind of mess I might find. What I found was no major damage to the fence, car, or Uncle except that he was hopping mad. He accused me of drinking too much wine and absolutely rejected any blame for the lever's being pulled down into drive. I left without the directions, with Uncle still chewing on me, but thankful that no major damage had been inflicted on anyone or anything.

Once, getting awfully low on gas, I made the mistake of telling Uncle we were almost out. From then on, since it was night, he felt every bright light we passed should be investigated to see if it were a gas station.

"Turn here, turn there," he'd command. If a car passed us going the opposite direction, he'd demand that I "blink your lights at them! Maybe they'll stop and give us some gas."

We did run out twice in the two years Uncle traveled with me. One happened on the Nestucca River Road between Hebo and Valley Junction. It was a rather cold winter day and fortunately the car chugged and coughed to a halt right in front of a kindly logger's home. He drove me down to the nearest service station about five miles away. We even got back before Uncle, who remained in the car, knew that I was gone. The other time we were between Oregon City and Tualatin on Highway 205. An attractive, petite highway patrol officer stopped and though state budget cuts were in effect, that should have limited the assistance officers were able to give, she stuck with us until we got the help we had to have. In fact, Uncle and I found helpful folk from every corner of our territory and in almost every walk of life. In many ways, to be in need affords opportunities for others to reach out that otherwise would be unavailable.

Speaking of driving down the road and some of Uncle's and my adventures, I must mention at this point his attitude toward those who shared those roadways with us. It seemed that he felt we always had the right of way. Uncle had no patience for slowness or for those he labeled inept drivers. At times, he would holler and shout angrily at any or all who got in what he considered "our way." Though he loved women with a respectful passion, he also felt that they had absolutely no sense when they got behind the wheel of an automobile. His own driving record was flawless until he was in his seventies, when he had a couple of close calls. Then he did something I've never heard of an older person doing. He wrapped up his license in a letter and sent it in to the Oregon Department of Motor Vehicles, saying in effect that he was no longer going to be driving. They examined his driving record, which included no accidents or tickets, and promptly sent his license back to him. They said anyone with a record as good as his could keep driving. When Uncle got it back, he returned it again. So did the Department of Motor Vehicles. Only after the third time did they keep his license. From then on, Uncle took the bus, an occasional taxi, or hitched a ride from friends or family.

We were in Shed, Oregon, where I'd already sold a 6,000 gallon tank to Jack Pugh. I was now working out the final details on a sale to his former herdsman who had gone into dairying on his own. Berniece was with me, along with Uncle, and he finally had had as long a stay in one place as he'd cared to. As usual, he started honking the horn. Berniece quickly came to what she hoped was my rescue by saying, "Don't do that, Uncle. That's how Gary makes us a living, by selling those tanks."

"Oh, phooey!" snorted Uncle. "If he hasn't sold 'em yet, he never will!" And with that, he gave three more sharp blasts on the horn.

Though I preferred a public restroom at a roadside park or service station, when Uncle had to go there often wasn't enough time to make it to one of those civilized facilities. On one such occasion, we were some twenty miles to the closest toilet and by the urgency in Uncle's voice I knew even half that distance was too far. I turned into the driveway of Glenn and Paula Barr's house and knocked on their door. The house was a newly-built, spacious ranch style, nestled into the hillside overlooking their farm and the surrounding valley. When Pauline came to the door and I explained the situation, she said, "Sure, bring Uncle right on in."

I got Uncle out of the car, across the lawn, up the steps, through the open door, and into the living room. We passed her number one son and his girlfriend, who were sprawled out on the couch. Next, we went by Glenn, who was sitting at the kitchen table. Then we took a hard left down the hall. Finally, with Paula pointing the way, we maneuvered another left into the bathroom. I got Uncle situated on the toilet, showed him where the paper was, and then left him to take care of his business while I took care of mine. Several minutes later, as

Glenn, Paula and I were discussing some dairy-related subjects, out came Uncle. I heard him as he moved down the hall and hurried to meet him half-way. He took my elbow and just as we turned the corner, Uncle came to an abrupt stop and said in a rather belligerent tone, "You must have a leaky pipe in there and you better get it fixed, because there is water all over the place!"

I was beside myself. I knew water hadn't been all over the place when I helped Uncle into the bathroom, so I could only assume Uncle had goofed something up. Without saying much of anything, I hastily propped Uncle up against the wall and rushed into the bathroom to check things out. What I found was that the bathroom looked like it had when I'd deposited Uncle there in the first place. I went back out, reassuring the Barr's that all was well. I turned to gather Uncle; I noticed that he was soaked from the front belt line of his trousers almost to the knees. Uncle must have pulled up his trousers, popped out his pecker from its pouch, and as he was sitting there peed all over himself. The Barr's were very understanding, saying very little as Uncle and I shuffled out the same way we came in, got in the car, and drove off. I later was able to get the pouch repositioned, and once my senses became dulled to the strong aroma of ripe urine, a couple of hours had gone by, his pants had dried, and I could hardly smell or see anything abnormal. As a matter of fact, with Uncle "normal" was the "abnormal" and as often as not, Uncle's appropriate advice turned out to be inappropriate.

Though Uncle meant well, his advice wasn't always based upon correct experience or reason. For example, after eating I'd often dry-brush my teeth, using a toothbrush I kept in the glove box.

"You better quit all that brushing," ordered Uncle. "Pyorrhea, puss, stink, and the whole works can happen because of all that brushing."

"Oh, yeah?" I retorted. "Since you're such an authority on taking care of teeth, how many of your own do you still have?"

"None," he confessed, falling silent.

"Well then," I'd continue, "You really aren't the one who can advise a person on how he should take care of his teeth!"

Sometimes he'd agree (we replayed this exchange many times) and I'd change the subject to something both of us were more comfortable with. It was interesting for me to note, however, that the last time I went to the dentist, he switched me to the softest-bristled brush available, saying I was scrubbing off part of the protective gum on some of my teeth. "This," said the dental hygienist, "could result in periodontal disease with all its unpleasant symptoms."

"Do you mean things like pyorrhea, puss, and foul odors?"

"Why, yes!" was the response of a somewhat surprised hygienist.

Uncle loved to relate to me the advice he gave some visitors who made a call on him one day while he was working at a port Blakley lumber mill. "They came to the company cabin I shared with a few other fellows. When I opened the door, there were about four or five Yapaneese fellas." They had seen Uncle's name on an employee roster and had come to meet the person who shared their ancestral name, Ono.

"Is Ono in?" asked his polite Oriental callers.

"Yes," replied Uncle. "That's me."

"You? Your name couldn't be Ono. You're not Japanese,"

replied the spokesman from the group.

By now Uncle was getting a bit irritated. "Calling me a liar, huh? Have you ever ever read the Bible?"

"No," replied the Japanese visitors.

"Well that figures!" barked Uncle. "You find one and read Nehemiah 7:37 and you'll find that the name Ono belonged to others way before you people ever laid claim to it. The last I saw of those fellows they turned on their heels and walked off talking Yapanese to themselves. Ha!"

At our church's annual corn feed, almost everyone made fools of themselves with his or her particular yodel or yell in the hog-calling contest. I was no exception. As the M.C., I undignified the most straight-laced members with such introductions as, "Lovable Libby and her litter yelp; Vivacious Verna with her varying voice; Jumping Judi and her jubilant gibberish; Cuddly Kelly and her cute cough; the Birch bellow; the happy Hanna holler; the Chris-cross crow; the Thomas toot; the Gibson growl; with the winner for the second year in a row being Sueeeee Sisco."

After the winner had been proclaimed, some asked Uncle how he'd call pigs. "Oh," said Uncle, "that's easy. I'd just take a bucket and throw in a few handfuls of corn and shake it. The Pigs would come a-running."

After both the laughter and a strong clamor for the prize that had already been given away to be taken back and given to Uncle died down, I asked him to tell the story about his hog-raising experiences. Uncle was ready and willing and plunged into the account. "It all started when a neighbor suggested he get a few pigs to clean up a worm-infested patch of corn that I'd grown."

"You'll not only clean up the corn," the neighbor said, "but you'll get some nice pork, too!"

"Well, that sounded just fine with me," continued Uncle. "So I bought the pigs and turned them loose into the corn patch. "Boy, oh boy, did they go at it. Day after day, they munched and rooted, growing so fat you could almost see the pounds go on. Towards the end, they'd just sit on their backsides and eat, so fat they'd hardly move. The corn finally ran out and, sure enough, I had some nice porkers, too! I called a butcher who said he could use some pork, but when he came out to look them over, he said, 'I can't take these pigs; they're too fat!'"

"Too fat?" I said. 'Well, what in the Vorld am I goin' to do with them?'"

"'Build a smoke house,' said the butcher. 'Dress out the hogs and hang them in it with a hot bed of coals underneath and smoke them. The pork won't be the best, but you'll still have some mighty fine eating.'"

"Well, I built the smoke house, butchered and hung the pigs inside, and then lit a small fire to begin the smoking process. All seemed to be going well until the heat from the fire started melting the fat on those huge hogs. The fat dripped onto the fire. Before anything could be done about it, the fire flared so wildly and the heat got so intense that the whole smokehouse burst into flames, burning itself and its contents completely up.

"The next year, on the advice of another, I got some more hogs to clean out a patch of Canadian thistle. 'They'll root them all out and rid the area of that pesky weed,' said the neighbor. Carefully I watched the pigs, withholding food from them much of the time so they wouldn't get too fat. Finally, the thistles were gone and I called the butcher. This time, he refused to buy them because they were too skinny. I finally just gave them away. First too fat, then too skinny. Boy, oh boy! I vowed never to raise another hog in my life, and I never did."

17

I TRUST YOU COMPLETELY, BUT PLEASE
SEND CASH

Uncle's condition for the next several days didn't outwardly seem to change, but to the careful, experienced observer, it was evident that he was losing ground. He couldn't keep his dentures in his mouth and without his teeth his speech was nearly impossible even for me to understand. Judi and I, Cathi and Berniece, though it was especially hard on them, visited Uncle regularly, as did Ruth and Esther. He seldom was out of bed, and all he seemed to want to do was sleep. We held his hand while we were there and he seemed to enjoy that, squeezing each one of us with an amazing amount of strength. Early one morning, I waved to Mr. Wall who motioned me on into his office. He invited me to sit down and after some small talk said he'd been in to see Uncle. He carefully selected words which in essence told me that Uncle was dying.

He explained that he and many others had found that sometimes a person needs permission or some type of release from those that he's closest to before he'd give up the struggle that life had become. We talked for some time, touching on our personal philosophies which included quite a bit of theology. I told him that I, too, felt Uncle was dying, but I wasn't sure that Uncle needed permission from anyone short of God Himself to do anything, including dying. We talked a bit more, and Mr. Wall changed the subject of the conversation by saying that the doctor had ordered care that made Uncle eligible for continued Medicare coverage, so the monetary requirements of his care for at least a couple more weeks would be minimal.

The Bible tells us that "the love of money is the root of all kinds of evil." It's also been said that money is a wonderful servant but a terrible master. One thing for sure, Uncle possessed no great passion for the accumulation of money. He never amassed a large quantity of it and was generous to others with the little he had, never getting overly concerned that his small savings were dwindling fast. When he came to live with us, he had less than $1,000 in his savings and wouldn't even have had that if it hadn't been for Ruth's generosity. She would often pay his insurance premiums, tax bills, and grocery bills out of her own pocket, just to make sure that Uncle's checks didn't bounce and that he could maintain a little savings.

He received a little over a hundred dollars a month Social Security, which didn't even cover his household expenses. The two years he lived with us, Ruth sent Uncle twenty dollars in cash every week as an allowance that he could do with as he pleased. The money arrived either Friday or Monday and was always one of the highlights of his week. It's amazing what a few dollars in one's pocket can do towards a feeling of self-worth, independence, and freedom. Part of his money he'd give away, often taking the whole bunch of us out for some pizza. Sometimes it would be, "Jerry, here's some money. Go out and buy me six bottles of beer." Once he said, "With all this traveling we do, we should have a compass!" Try as I might to dissuade him, he wouldn't rest until I found one for him. He put it in his pocket and to my knowledge never ever tried using it. But apparently there was security in knowing that if we needed a compass, it was there. I still have the thing, and whenever I see it, I'm reminded of that experience.

Uncle's biggest problem was that he knew he was supposed to get twenty dollars weekly, but he didn't always remember getting it. The very next day he may have spent all but a few dollars, but when he checked his wallet and only found a couple of dollars, he'd claim Ruth forgot, or, worse yet, he'd accuse whoever happened to be closest (usually me) of stealing from him.

I learned never to borrow anything of Uncle's, especially money. Once I did borrow five dollars, and he remembered for months that Jerry had borrowed money from him, but he forgot that I'd paid him back. He was generous with me, however, to a fault, and would often give me a few dollars for the simplest of services, refusing to take no for an answer. Some of the time, I'd have to sneak the money back into his wallet so that the next day he'd find at least something in his wallet when he'd eventually check.

Once in Sunnyside, Washington, we pulled into a service station to load up on gas and unload in the restroom. While the attendant filled up the car, I helped Uncle to the restroom. After I got him situated, I dashed out to the car to finish the transaction. The attendant looked at me through misty eyes and said, "It sure is nice to see a young man take care of an old person like you're doing." Wishing my reward to come from God and not man (or just to be ornery) I quickly replied, "If you were his only heir and he was worth $600,000 how would you treat him?"

183

Though at a loss for words for a moment, he collected himself and said, "I still think it's commendable."

I thanked him and confided, "He's really not worth that much," and then briefly told him about our travels together. I really think our stop made his day.

18

OLD NORWEGIANS NEVER DIE, (ONO, ONO, ONO!)

After finishing my conversation with Mr. Wall, I went down to Uncle's room. Uncle appeared to be lying in exactly the same position as he'd been the day before. I talked with him as if he could hear and understand each word, and perhaps he could. I told him about the dairymen I'd seen since I'd last been in. I held his hand and he responded with his usual tight clasp. Remembering Mr. Wall's advice, before leaving I got up from the chair beside his bed and bent low to his ear. "Uncle," I said, "we love you and have enjoyed having you live with us in our home. You've been a real help to me and good company on the road. It may be that God is now ready to take you to be with Him now. It's all right with me if you want to go. Say hello to my mother when you get up there. I love you, Uncle." I gave his hand a hard squeeze and then added, "I'm leaving now, Uncle. I'll be back in the morning." I leaned a little closer and gave Uncle a kiss on his forehead, gently pried my hand from his, and backed away from his bedside, around the curtain that separated him from his roommate, and turned and left the room.

Uncle didn't die that night or for the next few days. I never mentioned death to him again. About three days later, we got a telephone call from the nursing supervisor, who said that she felt Uncle wouldn't last through the night. It was already quite late when I arrived and pulled up a chair beside his bed. I held his hand, which had lost none of its strength, but each breath sounded as if it could be his last. At times, it appeared he'd stopped, but then his chest would resume its heaving. I told him how much we all loved him, but apart from his tight hold on my hand, there was no response. Next to Uncle just dropping off beside me in the car, this was the way I'd have wanted his long life to end. I stayed right beside him for several hours, with a staff member checking in on us once in a while. Finally, it became obvious that his death wasn't as imminent as the staff first thought. At about 2:00am, I gave Uncle a pat and another squeeze and said I'd be back later in the morning.

Uncle hung on for three more days before taking his last breath. The morning he died, I had to go into Tigard to pick up some materials for a handyman project I had going at the house. As I drove by the Care Center, I decided I'd stop and see Uncle on my way home. About an hour later, I swung into the King City Care Center, parked, and walked in as I had dozens of times. Uncle's wing was one of the furthest that headed off in a somewhat southwesterly direction. I got to his room, walked past his roommate, who nodded, and then past the partially-pulled curtain that separated the two beds. Uncle looked the same, except his color was a bit more ashen. I reached out and took his hand; it felt rather cool but not cold. "Uncle," I called. But his open eyes were unresponsive. I couldn't detect any breathing. I gently shook him, as you would try to awaken someone from a deep sleep. Still no response. I picked up his right arm, as he was facing me lying somewhat on his left side. It was rather stiff and resisted my pull. Then I noticed a residue of something like a baby spits up that had come out of the left corner of his mouth. Uncle was gone. I knew it. I gently laid his arm back down and walked out of his room, down the hall to the nursing station. The overworked and underpaid charge nurse politely asked if she could help me.

"My Uncle, Charles Ono, I believe has passed away."

She looked startled and the said, "I'll get the nurse who's in charge of that wing."

I turned and walked back to Uncle's room, getting there at the same time as the nurse who had just been called. She was extremely nervous and quick to recount her recent contact with Uncle. How he'd eaten some that morning and seemed to be fine. She said she'd been busy with everyone else, but it hadn't been that long since she'd last checked in on him. We walked to his bed and she quickly wiped the corner of his mouth and placed the stethoscope to his chest. She checked his pulse and, finding none, said, "Yes, he'd died. Would you like to stay in here with him for a while?"

"No," I said calmly. "I'll go make a couple of phone calls."

"Okay," she said. "I'll clean him up and then you can check back here if you'd like."

"Thank you," I said "You've all done so much for Uncle."

Judi was at work, so I didn't get in touch with her and ended up making only one call at the pay phone near the nurses' station. It was to Ruth. When Ruth answered, I told her that Uncle had passed away. Her response was concern for me and a reiteration that he'd been ready and that his struggles were now over. She assured me that the Care

Center knew what to do with the remains and that she'd get back in touch with me concerning the details of his funeral.

I went home to an empty house, and late that afternoon, when Judi came home from work, picking up the girls on the way, who'd been shopping, I told them Uncle had died. There were some tears, followed by a lot of reminiscing. The girls took it quite well. In my estimation, their reaction was due to a lot of preparation on both Judi's and my part. For us now, as psychologists call it, a significant emotional event had taken place. Just as when Uncle first came to live with us, his death would require new adjustments to be made, again changing our lifestyle. We wouldn't revert back to "Before Uncle," but rather regroup, tighten up ranks depleted by one, and press on in our journey through life with greater understanding and purpose, knowing we've been enriched and are better equipped because of Uncle.

Just as the Bible says, "O, death, where is your sting . . .?" (1 Corinthians 15:55), for Uncle, death wasn't something to fear. Some older people I've known never talked of death and did everything they could think of to avoid the subject and prolong the inevitable. However, Uncle talked of his own death and those of others as most people discuss the weather. Though a scrapper even to the end, it wasn't uncommon when things weren't going the way he wanted for Uncle to say, "I can't understand why the Lord doesn't take me home. I give to Billy Graham, to several missionaries, and belong to the Bible-A-Month Club, but He just leaves me here. I wonder what I've done wrong?"

All my friends knew and loved Uncle, but sometimes they were completely taken aback by his frankness and open honesty. Erhardt

Steinborn, a good friend I'd grown up with, was on the receiving end of those types of words more than once. Erhardt lived on a large farm on Highway 99, just before you turn off if you're coming from the north to get to our place. When we first moved out to Sherwood to live in a house built in part out of an old barn, we weren't aware that Erhardt lived anyplace close. It had been over twenty years since I'd left my home town of Ferndale, Washington, up on the Canadian border in northwestern Washington, and it was there that I'd last seen Erhardt. Sometime after I'd left, industry had moved into the area near where Erhardt was farming with his parents and had eventually purchased their farm. They relocated, unknown to me, in Sherwood in the early '70's. After we had moved to Sherwood, we would go back and forth on the highway past the Steinborn farm, not realizing who owned it. Finally, after three years, through a mutual friend, I learned of its ownership. In a matter of hours, I contacted Erhardt and we were able to revive our friendship. Now I usually stop by at least a couple of times a week, and Erhardt and Freta, his mother (his father passed away shortly after their move from Ferndale), have been a constant source of pleasure to us. They always have coffee on, and Freta, a cook par excellence, usually provides cake or cookies, and often a full meal, to go along with it.

Towards the end of Uncle's trips with me, he'd seldom get out of the car and this was even true at the Steinborn's', one of his favorite stops. This restriction, however, didn't stop Erhardt's or Freta's hospitality one little bit. They'd simply fix up a plate or wrap up a warm goodie in a napkin and bring it out to Uncle along with his coffee. The occasion I have in mind began like many others. Erhardt had brought out some coffee and cake when Uncle then motioned him closer and said, "I'm not going to be around much longer, but you remember this. When I do go, I'm going to put in a good word for you." We all chuckled then, but it wasn't too many more weeks until Uncle was gone. I'm sure that if the Lord allowed the "good words" for Freta and Erhardt they would have had the way to Heaven partially paved for them by Uncle. The truth of the matter is that none of us are or can be good enough. Heaven is an unearned gift from God through our faith in the person and work of Jesus Christ. But, true faith is accompanied by good works so Erhardt and Freta will be rewarded.

Like most of us, Uncle hated cancer. Yet modern medicine has known for years that several types of cancer can now be controlled or even cured. To Uncle, any cancer meant a sure, quick, and painful death. His mother went with it when he was just a boy. He seemed to relish telling of one brother who, in spite of Uncle's urging, postponed having a sore on his cigarette-stained lip taken care of. By the time he finally went to the doctor, it was too late. Uncle vividly described how the cancerous sore ate away his brother's face.

"Boy, oh boy, did it stink!" he'd say with a certain morbid satisfaction. "But me, the doctor went through my blood thoroughly and didn't find one single cancer cell."

Toward the end of Uncle's long life, his death was sometimes prematurely reported. I'd stopped at a 7-11 store to use the telephone, but I was close enough to the car to overhear some teenagers who had cut classes for a Coke and smoke break. As they walked by the Volare, I overheard one say, "He's dead. I'm sure he's dead! Look he doesn't move at all." They stood there for several minutes trying to spot any movement – a heaving chest, a slight movement of a limb – but there was nothing. Finally, they called off their vigil or wake, having convinced themselves that my dozing Uncle had in fact gone to his reward.

Along the same line, one of my daughter's friends who had seen Uncle sitting in my car many times had a similar response. She'd never seen Uncle move either, so she finally came to a conclusion and told it to Berniece, "What's wrong, can't you face reality? You are hauling around a dead person, trying to pass him off as alive." Berniece, of course, knew better and just tried to make light of a very unusual sight.

Speaking of death, just before Uncle's first wife died, her last request was that Uncle look after her widowed best friend, Karla. Uncle agreed, fulfilling his promise by marrying Karla. They lived together for many years, Karla once remarking to a friend, "I never knew it was possible to have someone love me so much." She, like Uncle's first wife, suffered from hardening of the arteries and ended up, for the last couple years of her life, unable to care for herself. She was totally dependent upon Uncle, but no person in her condition had it so good. Finally, after close to two years, he called Ruth and confessed, "I don't think I can care for Karla anymore. We'd better consider putting her in a home." The next morning, as Uncle was carrying her from their bathroom to her bed, she died in his arms.

Sometime later, Uncle asked Ruth, who had never married and was living with her sister, to trip down the aisle with him. He was then in his late eighties and she was quite a few years younger. Ruth graciously turned down the offer, saying that her sister needed continual care, so marriage was out of the question. Uncle didn't like her refusal one bit and always thereafter complained how Esther just lay up there in her bed, listening to the radio and reading to find ideas on new illnesses to try when she got over the present one. This she did, Uncle claimed, so that she'd have Ruth's undivided attention forever. As a result of this opinion, Uncle wasn't always as pleasant towards Esther as he could be, but he always worshipped the ground Ruth walked on, in spite of his spurned proposal.

While I'm on the subject of death, and due to the fact that I don't know of a better place to put this, I want to get in a few strokes for the nursing home industry. Though, like any business, it has some shortcomings, by and large nursing home staffs consist of a dedicated group of people who are performing an extremely valuable service. Most whom I've talked to realize there are better ways to provide for old folks, but too many people haven't many options available to them. I don't know how we could have coped with Uncle's care in our home if Mike Adams, owner of Elenbaas Dairy Supply, hadn't allowed me to take Uncle along on company business out on the road. I venture to guess it would have had to be a nursing home much earlier, since there aren't many employers like him around. Anyway, while Uncle was in the King City Care Center, he received excellent care.

This kindness was especially true of one young girl named Dawn on the housekeeping staff. She attended our church, so she had met Uncle there, but I'm sure even if she hadn't, she'd have felt the same way about him. I say that because I'd heard her talk in a very loving way many times about many other people in the center. Hired only to make beds, sweep the floors, and clean up messes, Dawn would still spend her breaks with patients. Often she'd work especially hard and fast so that she'd be able to take a little extra time with those she'd come to be especially fond of. She provided love and attention that couldn't have been bought with any amount of money. For example, she'd talk with Uncle, hold his hand, pat and rub him, feed him, and shower him with kisses.

When uncle died, the funeral was fortunately on her day off, because she'd have done whatever necessary to be there. She rode along with us, being included in the two services and the two meals that were to cap off the day. During the graveside service she took a number of snapshots of everything from the grave and casket to the hearse and headstone. Uncle, I'm sure, would have approved.

Since Uncle didn't want to carry a grudge with him to the grave over Esther's standing in the way of his marrying her sister, Ruth and Esther both were named the heirs to his estate. This had been decided by Uncle way before he ever came to live with us and fitted the years of unselfish devotion and care which they provided Uncle. They, in turn, have made provision that when Uncle's modest house is sold, the only possession that had much value, we will receive a generous share to assist in the education of our daughters. These details weren't to be the last word on the settling of Uncle's estate, however.

Hearing that Uncle had died, two of his relatives living in Norway wrote Ruth and Esther, asking if they had been remembered in Uncle's will. Uncle had visited them during his mid-1970's Scandinavian trip and had apparently left the impression that he was a man of significant means. One cousin even went so far as to request the Norwegian Consulate in the Portland area check into the matter, to make sure she hadn't been illegally overlooked. In fairness, the older of the two simply asked if there wasn't some money she could pass along to a young relative who had been of real assistance to her in a time of need. I'm sure that if Uncle could see what was happening after his death, he would enjoy every bit and piece of the issues surrounding the settling of his "estate."

19

WISDOM IS A WHOLE LOT OF COMMON SENSE

R uth called the night of Uncle's death and told me that all had gone well with the proper mortuary picking up Uncle's remains, and if it would be possible, we could meet with the funeral director to finalize all the arrangements the next day. "That would be fine with me," I agreed. Then, after asking how Judi and the girls were taking the news, she went on to outline in a very precise manner the details of how the funeral was to be handled. She asked my approval, or for suggestions on matters she hadn't been too sure about. I could tell that little else had occupied her from the moment she first heard. She had contacted the church and arranged for the preacher, telling him that she also wanted me to say a few words. With this responsibility in view, I reflected on memories of Uncle, sifting through some of the things I'd jotted down that would be both interesting and appropriate.

One of the things about Uncle that would be of interest would be a few of the, by now, famous quotes Uncle had shared along the way. For example, once after soup, pie, and coffee at our local restaurant, The Sherwood Peddler, we'd almost made it to the car after finishing when Uncle stumbled slightly. I caught him, and really he'd been in no danger of falling, but before I knew what was happening, a passenger door of the van parked right beside us flew open and a middle-aged woman (lower middle, if you'd compare her age to Uncle's) rushed out and around the car, insisting that she help Uncle into his seat. I helped with the door and she gently lowered Uncle into his place.

"There you are, sweety," she cooed, and then went on with, "Now isn't that nice, sweety? Are you comfortable, sweety?" Once she was sure he was seated and comfortable, she hugged him and planted a big kiss smack dab on his mouth saying, "bye-bye, sweety." Then she left almost as fast as she came.

As we were driving away, I said, "Now wasn't that nice, Uncle? You got some help, a huge hug, and a big kiss."

"Ah, yes," said Uncle. "But tell me something. How in the Vorld did she know I was Scandinavian?"

"Scandinavian?" I asked.

"Yes," he replied. "She kept calling me 'Swedy'."

We all knew patience wasn't one of Uncle's virtues, so it's appropriate that his most famous quote was provoked by that fact. We were at the Vellinga dairy on Tone Road in Tillamook. Uncle, who'd been watching me explain the virtues of our fine product to Joe (at that time the chairman of the board of directors for the Tillamook cheese plant) finally got tired of waiting. He'd sat patiently for quite a while, but finally he figured he'd studied the same scenery long enough. With quick, jerky motions, using both hands, he rolled down the window and with the dairyman and me both just a few feet away bellowed, "Get a yes or no outta that guy and let's get the hell out of here!" Though I didn't get the "yes" right then, several weeks later I did, and I never talked with Joe or his son, Leon, again that they didn't mention the incident or comment on Uncle.

Uncle had a definition for everything, and it often wasn't the same as anyone else's. When he suffered from excessive gas, he's simply raise up a bit on one cheek and let fly, assuring all and sundry, "It's nothing but a little stomach gas escaping." A quick roll-down of the window for a few minutes would usually take care of the results, but several times when the aroma would linger, I knew I'd better stop and check for lumps in his shorts.

20

MUCH ADO ABOUT SOMEONE

The next day after Uncle's death, at the appointed time, Cathi, Berniece and I (Judi had to work and couldn't go) picked up Ruth and Esther and headed over to the mortuary. Ruth and Esther were dressed to the hilt and seemed almost in a festive mood. Even Esther, who only makes it out to the most important of events, was caught up in the excitement of the hour. Though we'd made no effort to shelter our girls from the cold reality of death, this was the first time they'd ever been involved in making the arrangements for someone's funeral.

We parked in the empty lot of the funeral home and went through the big glass door and into the plush, traditionally-furnished waiting room. Nobody came out right away, so after a few minutes, I started poking around to see if I could find someone. There must have been a bell or buzzer that had sounded some place, because before I found anyone, the funeral director found me. After introducing myself, I led the way back to where I'd left my daughters and Ruth and Esther.

They'd been enjoying each other's company and had a lively conversation going when we reached them. The funeral director introduced himself and as he ushered us into his immaculate office,

Ruth and Esther, both talking at the same time, started explaining all the details of who we were and the wonderful job we'd done in taking care of Uncle. They laid it on especially thick about me, and while one was catching her breath the other would push on, giving her special version and often not waiting for the other to finish. Before everyone had been seated, enough words had been spoken to handle sufficiently the arrangements for any dozen normal internments. Once seated with Ruth, Esther and I nestled in between and directly in front of the mortician's mammoth desk and the girls seated together to our left on an overstuffed leather couch, the man spoke.

"Let's get some details down in writing, and the first thing we should do is prepare an obituary for the newspaper," he suggested.

Almost in unison, Ruth and Esther rattled off all the living relatives, finishing the whole list before either had to take a breath. The funeral director had made an attempt to list the first name mentioned, but must have actually only gotten a couple of letters down before he'd lost his train of thought in the spate of confusing names. He sat there with a polite expression frozen on his face, pen in mid-air, and I could sense that he wished he'd called in sick that day.

In typical monotone and controlled modulation of accepted mortician's form, the director broke in on some of the extra details that were by now being added saying, "Let's start with surviving brothers and sisters and move slowly through the whole group again. Now, first of all, does he have any surviving brothers or sisters?"

"No, of course not. Do you realize he was almost a hundred years old? And he was one of the last to be born of all of his immediate family. They all have been dead for many years."

So it went with piling up in-depth details, much of which I'd never even heard, spelling and re-spelling each and every name, disagreeing several times on minor points about the person or place until one would concede and the director would hastily write the bit down.

We finally got down where part of our family should be mentioned, and we went round and round on merely using my deceased mother's name to give blanket recognition to the survival of her family. The director felt that "the Berniece Gorsuch family" was inappropriate for the newspaper but would be fine to use in the church's funeral service program. Being not that concerned with appropriateness, I made one final feeble attempt to have the notice worded that way in the newspaper, too, but got no support from the decision-makers, though Cathi and Berniece were nodding their approval. I acquiesced. With a few negative comments about including Uncle's stepson (who hadn't given the support that Ruth and Esther felt he should have), that part of the arrangement had been made.

We next went through a few details on the service itself, picking out two dates and times just in case one didn't prove to be satisfactory. Decisions were made about death certificates, the place of the services, and the cemetery procedures. The Lutheran church right across the street from the funeral home and a short grave-side service for the family only were settled on, and a few final, incidental details were worked out. Then, with the skill of a seasoned veteran, the director moved inoffensively into the financial commitment. Much of this cost would be determined by the casket and grave-liner selections, with the other services and fees already having been determined. Uncle had some insurance that would help in part, so his company and policy information were exchanged and we were ready for the next step – selecting the casket.

We all trooped upstairs to a big room to view, displayed very neatly, a cross-section of almost every casket that was made, from cardboard to copper. Ruth had stated from the start that she was going to make up the difference between what the insurance paid and the actual cost of the entire service. Knowing Uncle as well as I did from two years of almost continuous contact, I knew he would have picked for himself one of the least expensive caskets and I made sure Ruth understood that and didn't feel pressured into over-spending. The director stood in the background, allowing for our privacy, but close enough to answer any questions. Cathi and Berniece looked over each and every one, not with uncle in mind but rather simply out of youthful curiosity. I liked the look of natural wood, but wouldn't pick it out for Uncle or anyone else for that matter. Finally, Ruth called me over and showed me a couple she was interested in – a bronze and a silver-colored steel, both with white interiors. I said I preferred the silver, but if it was me, I would buy one not quite so expensive. She felt it wouldn't be too much, liked the silver also, and informed the director that we'd decided.

The director was instantly by our sides, taking the card that had been lying on the pillow to make sure our selection was reserved for us. Then, we climbed back down the stairs with the man and into the office, where we sat down one more time. A few quick punches on his calculator tabulated the final figures, and we agreed on the method of payment. Then, we exchanged a very few additional words about when the remains would be ready for viewing and the times that would be appropriate to tell people when they could come by. We thanked the director and went back out through the same big glass door through which we'd entered the mortuary earlier out into the sunshine and, except for our car, an empty parking lot.

At one point during our arrangement experience, the secretary from Uncle's Lutheran church directly across the street had come into the director's office and introduced herself. She assisted in arranging for songs, appropriate Scripture reading, and musicians, and told us that immediately following the services, the ladies of the church would have a nice luncheon for all the family. She then left with a parting invitation to stop by the church after the arrangements had been completed to take a look at where the service was scheduled to be held. We had accepted the invitation, so now we went directly over to the church. After trying a couple of locked doors, I found an open one and we let ourselves in. The secretary was quickly by our sides and took us from the kitchen to the auditorium, pointing out all unique details of their huge and beautiful building. I felt Uncle would be pleased to use this place for his "send off".

21

A HERE'S THE CHURCH AND HERE'S THE
STEEPLE, OPEN THE DOORS AND SEE . . .
UNCLE

U ncle's church was extremely important to him, and though he expressed no interest in joining our little fellowship of believers, he seldom missed a service.

Christmas of 1977 found our whole family, including Uncle, who was just out for a visit, going to church. Uncle insisted on sitting right up front so he was less likely to not miss a word. The church was packed. People had come out of the proverbial woodwork to fill every pew. All went well until just a few minutes before the close of the service. Then, Uncle leaned over to me and, in his very "quiet" voice which only three or four pews of folks behind us could hear, said, "Say, tell me something. Do you have a toilet in this place?"

Knowing that the minister was almost through, I leaned over to Uncle and answered right into his ear, "Can you hold it for a few minutes, Uncle? The service is just about over."

Uncle, not having heard a single word I'd spoken, assumed I hadn't heard him. "I said," he stated firmly, in his regular voice that everyone in the entire congregation could hear, "do you have a toilet in this place?! I've got to urinate!"

The minister stopped speaking, and after a couple long seconds of silence, light laughter rippled throughout the entire church. Resigned to my fate, I helped Uncle to his feet. As we turned and walked down the center aisle in what this time was dead silence, I heard, over my shoulder, the minister chuckle, "This is the first time I've ever seen an invitation in reverse."

Uncle usually enjoyed going to church, but once in a while, he felt a bit too comfortable in his chair or bed. I'd say to him, "Would you like to go to church with us this morning, Uncle?"

"No," he'd reply quite emphatically. He'd then would just sit or lie there without saying another word. It wouldn't be long, however, before he'd call me over and say, "Well, I'd better go with you. I don't have a good excuse, so I guess I'll come. Give me a hand and help me get ready."

I'd get him and myself dressed, and then the two of us would go out to the car and sit for ten minutes or so, waiting for Judi and the girls to finish getting ready. On the way, we'd usually pick up Florence, the eighty-plus-year-old widow lady and her granddaughter, Kelly, and then continue on to what Uncle called, "The Little Church on the Prairie." Once we'd parked, I'd assist Uncle into the building to a special place in the foyer. It was centrally located and had a straight shot down the aisle to the pulpit and platform. Doug Wilcox, our "sound man", had fixed up for Uncle a pair of earphones with which he was able to tune in to first the adult Sunday School class and later to the morning service.

I taught the adult class for quite a while, and it was not uncommon to have Uncle comment on what I'd said. He couldn't have heard the class without the earphones, but his spot was close enough so that the rest of us could hear almost every move Uncle made. Though he often slept during much of the class, when he was awake, not much went by him. We often heard such full-voiced comments as "I don't believe that!" or "Who in the vorld is that speaking? Whatever he's saying, I'm sure he didn't get that out of the Bible!" The class would laugh, and I'd continue on with something like, ". . . and furthermore the Bible says . . ."

Uncle's earphones weren't working properly one Sunday. Try as we might, we couldn't get them to work. He grumbled, moaned, and groaned. Finally thinking it somehow was the speaker's fault, he said, "They should send that guy to the Salvation Army. They'd put him on a street corner and teach him how to speak up."

Even when the earphones worked perfectly, Uncle often didn't hear much. One Sunday, during a time when we were without a pastor, we had a guest speaker. As it turned out, we invited the man back to candidate for the position subsequently calling him to be our full-time minister. If we'd left the decision up to Uncle, however, that first time would have been his last. Now, in fairness to the speaker, Uncle's evaluation was not based on a thorough appraisal of his abilities. Uncle would often doze through most of a sermon. Then, depending on what part he'd heard, he'd make his judgment.

Pastor Carl's first sermon didn't impress Uncle. After the service, within easy earshot of Carl, Uncle reached out, rapped Libby Hanna on the legs with his cane, and motioned her over to him. Then, in a full voice which people thirty feet away could hear, Uncle said, "Now wasn't that the worst sermon you've ever heard in all your life?"

Embarrassed, Libby didn't know what to say, so while she was thinking, Uncle (who assumed she hadn't heard) raised his voice and repeated, "I said, wasn't that the worst sermon you've ever heard?!" I got Uncle up and hustled him out of there while the getting was good. Try as I might in the weeks that followed, during which Carl became our Pastor, Uncle never came out with a critique even remotely close to a world's worst. Each Sunday after that, as I passed by Carl with Uncle hanging onto my arm with one hand and his cane with the other, I'd sweetly inquire of Uncle, "What did you think of the sermon today?" Each time his response was the same, "Fine, very fine. Couldn't have been better." I'd say, "Ah, shucks!" to myself as Uncle continued to congratulate the minister.

Once our church deacon board, which included me, decided to go to the beach for a Sunday afternoon and Monday retreat. Its purpose was to get away and give our undivided attention to some church administration needs, as well as to have a time of fellowship together. We went to Ken and Riva Sisco's cabin in Manzanita, west of Nehalem and a few miles south of Cannon Beach. The men knew that, as Uncle said, "Where Jerry goes I go," so there was no question that Uncle would be part of the group. The cabin was small and modest but comfortable and equipped with everything we needed. All went quite well. I say "quite" well because there were several times when Uncle, whose eyesight was better than his hearing, accused us of having a meeting where everybody just sat in a circle looking at the ceiling but saying nothing. Then, since Uncle couldn't hear anybody, though there was a lot of talking going on and he was sitting right beside the fire that was cracking away in the fireplace, he got the campfire spirit and started rattling off all kinds of yarns. Try as I might to explain to him that we were discussing business, he just brushed me off, told me I was crazy, and continued spinning his tall tales. We did the best we could to continue on until about 10:00pm. Finally, we decided to call it a night and began dividing up the sleeping areas.

The cabin had two bedrooms with a couple of beds in each room and two day couches in the living room. Not realizing what we'd been doing and where we'd be staying the night, Uncle turned to me when everyone, including the cabins' owner, was still seated in the circle, and said, "Say, Jerry, tell me something. Where are we going to spend the night?"

"Right here," I replied.

Immediately, with raised voice, his response was, "What? In this rat hole?" It took several minutes for most of us to stop laughing. As for me, who'd caught the initial reaction of the owner, I'm still laughing.

Finally, things settled down, everyone took care of his pre-bedtime chores, and all, including Uncle and me, were tucked in. Someone flipped the last light off, and the talking began to taper off. Just before it stopped altogether, with everyone still awaiting the sandman, Uncle came through one last time, "Say, Jerry, tell me something. Are there any women here tonight?" Now the talking quit altogether. Everybody was listening. What, I thought is Uncle going to come up with this time? It sounded like our minister had even stopped breathing, and everyone else also was making sure he wouldn't miss a syllable.

"No," I said. "There aren't any women here tonight."

"It figures," Uncle muttered. "It takes a woman to know how to make a bed up right!" We all chuckled, and I breathed a sigh of relief.

Ninety-eight-year-old Uncle was often the center of attention, and people would go out of their way to say good morning and or offer him a bit of encouragement. Once on the way out of church, a fortyish blond well-wisher greeted Uncle enthusiastically, asking how he was doing. Uncle responded in good form with his usual, "Fine, fine. I couldn't be better." We proceeded out the door, making a left turn on our way out to the parking lot and our car. We hadn't gone four steps after the turn when Uncle came to a complete stop. He turned and said to me, "Say, tell me. Who was that Old Lady?" I couldn't let that one get away, so after delivering Uncle safely to the car, I rushed back into the church and informed Mrs. Fortyish of Uncle's words. I hadn't meant to offend her, but I could tell that's exactly what I'd done. I then got back into her good graces, I think, by explaining that if Uncles remark hadn't been so ridiculous, I wouldn't have shared it with her, thus giving her a back-handed compliment. Since it was she who, with her husband Ken, owned the beach cabin which Uncle had complained about earlier, she should have by now been used to my sense of humor. I now always refer to their cabin as Riva's Rat Hole.

Though Uncle often criticized the way I taught my Sunday School classes, I'm sure he would have approved of the ways I handled a question that came up about circumcision. I say that because it was his direct, straight-forward example in handling sensitive situations that gave me the courage to tackle this one head-on. After fielding the question "What's circumcision?" I threw it back at the class by asking, "How many know what circumcision is?" Not a soul raised his or her hand or acknowledged the question positively in any way. Of course, I would have gotten the same answer if I'd asked for the hands of those who didn't know what circumcision was. But that would have been the easy way out and not worthy of the example Uncle had been setting for me.

I took a deep breath (Uncle wouldn't have, but I'm still learning), picked up a piece of chalk, turned my back on the mixed group of ten high schoolers (something else Uncle wouldn't have done), and drew a phallus, complete with foreskin. Quickly adding that they weren't this big, I then proceeded to explain how a Jewish priest took the male infant at eight days old, the perfect biological time for rapid healing, and cut around the end of the phallus to eliminate its shroud of skin. From that point on, every time the male relieved himself, he would have before him a reminder that he as an individual and collectively as a nation was different, of a special people, chosen of God. I turned around to wide eyes that quickly looked down or away, got no response to "Any questions: and moved on, knowing that Uncle would have been proud of me.

During a church picnic that was held at our place, the whole flock, many of whom were tee-totallers, were gathered around ready to dive into the food as soon as grace was said. In the hush just prior to the prayer, Uncle boomed out, "Say, Yudi! Tell me something?" Everybody bent a sanctimonious ear and waited in reverential awe for the wonderful words of wisdom that would proceed from the lips of this loving, aged saint. "Do you have any beer in the house?" Jay Duffus, a fine gentleman and understanding individual, was our pastor at the time, and to show that he didn't begrudge Uncle a cool one, asked him to lead us in the blessing on the food. Uncle agreed and waxed very eloquent, re-establishing his piety with even the most tee-totaling souls who had flinched at the earlier remark.

Later, after Uncle had eaten his fill, he left the back deck where everybody had gathered to eat, went inside and down the spiral stairs for a nap in his family-room sleeping quarters. I followed, and thus happened to witness an interesting confrontation. Upon arriving at his fold-up hide-a-bed couch, much to his dismay, he found that six-foot-three Mick had beaten him to it. It was quite a sight, since Mick didn't even come close to fitting. His feet stuck out about fourteen inches past the armrest over which his legs were laid. His right arm had fallen from his chest to lie limply on the floor. His mouth was wide open, shadowed by the hat balanced on his forehead. He was snoring loudly. Uncle stood with cane poised, frozen in unbelief that someone would dare violate his territory. I watched as he finally swung into action, jabbing his cane at the sleeping giant. Finally, one eye opened and then the other, and Uncle, who under most any other circumstances would have been forgiving, bellowed, "Get out of my bed!"

Workdays were important way to take care of outside chores and general maintenance on the church. These chores would be tasks not covered by the normal duties of our janitor. Though Uncle wasn't expected to swing a paint brush or trim the shrubs or wash windows, he would come along with me anyway. I'd prop him up in a chair under a tree or on the covered walkway in front of the church. Sometimes he'd simply prefer sitting and snoozing in the car. When lunch time came, however, that was another story. Uncle wanted to be right in the thick of it. As he sat in the middle of the group of twenty or so, some of whom were sprawled out on the grass, Uncle motioned me over, apparently not remembering who I was, and confided, with everyone listening, "Say, my birthday's coming up in five days and people from all over the place will be sending me money. I would appreciate it if you'd instruct everybody to send it to my niece in Portland. I don't trust those people I live with!"

Fortunately, by now I was used to these lapses. Even though almost everyone had heard Uncle's remark, and those who didn't were quickly told, I could laugh with everybody else. One thing, though, that wasn't so funny were Uncle's prayers when he was upset. Often when he didn't get his way, or for whatever reason got to feeling sorry for himself, he'd sit in bed with his pancake hat-cap in place, covers pulled up to his chin, bow his head, clasp his hands across his midsection, and fervently pray, "Oh, Lord! Take me out of this mess." He'd then quote the entire Lord's Prayer, "Our Father which art in heaven . . . "word perfect.

Fortunately, though this happened many times, he'd more often thank the Lord for being so good to him. He'd rejoice in his good health in spite of the number of his years and their inherent disabilities. He'd often thank God for "Yudi and the girls" and even sometimes remember me. Finally, he was almost always a constant source of comfort and encouragement, and all of us inwardly suffered when he felt down. We all were glad his low spells didn't happen more than they did, for his usual "May the Lord Jesus Christ bless us all" was brimming with love and devotion and made us forget his and our own moments of unhappiness.

22

THE COLD HARD FACTS OF THE MATTER

After the tour, we left the church, thanking the secretary for her assistance so far and also for the help she was to provide in the days that followed (though this may not sound appropriate) to make the funeral a resounding success. Before heading back to Ruth and Esther's, we drove to the cemetery to find Uncle's plot. This always was a difficult task, even when Uncle was alive and shouting directions, "Turn here. Go that way. No, not there. It's across from where all the Gypsies are buried. Over near the Yapanese part of the cemetery. There's a big weeping willow right near the headstone." Finally, we'd find it.

This time, even after we got in the general vicinity, it took us almost fifteen minutes before I stumbled across the ground-level marker on which Gertrude, his first wife, was listed by birth and death. On the overlapping stone, Charles Neilson Ono was listed by birthdate, to which the 22nd of August, 1981 would be added to complete the inscription. We stood reminiscing for a while, and just before leaving, I took out my knife and cleaned the overlapping sod from around the stone.

We couldn't just drop Ruth and Esther off at their home and head for ours, not that we'd even want to. As usual, we ended up inside their home for an array of Scandinavian cookies, fruit and coffee or juice. We all had a delightful time, especially Ruth and Esther. They assured us they were extremely happy with the arrangements that had been made for Uncle.

The next day, Monday, was the first workday I would spend without at least coming back and sharing the day's events with a living, breathing Uncle. As it turned out, I wasn't going to give up that easily. Towards evening, after visiting a number of dairies (none of which I now can recall), I found myself very close to the funeral home. I remembered that the director said that Uncle would be ready for viewing Monday afternoon. At the time, I hadn't felt any desire to see his remains. I did now. So, I swung into the nearly empty and by now somewhat familiar parking lot. I walked in and, though I can't remember, must have been directed by someone into a viewing room. There I found Uncle's remains neatly arranged in the silver steel casket.

Soft music was playing as I walked up to view for the last time what had been, until a few days ago, a face that had remained unchanged for all thirty-seven years of my life. Though the embalmers knew their craft well and were true artisans, even their skills fell short. I've yet to see a corpse that really looked natural. I touched his hands and felt the skin's smoothness. Their texture felt the same, but their coolness brought back the reality of his death. I looked more intently at his face, noting how much they'd missed the life-like essence of his mouth. It was drawn out and straight and seemed much too wide. I smoothed my hands through his hair while at the same time noticing the makeup and powder. I wished he could lie there with his pancake hat on, but when I'd suggested it, the idea had been quietly rejected as unthinkable.

I whispered a prayer, not for Uncle but just to thank God that Uncle's struggles were over and for the first and now eternal time he was in perfect peace. As King David said when his firstborn son by Bathsheba died, "He can't come back to me, but I can go to him." Uncle was gone, but his memories would outlive me, and one of these days, I'll go to him. I left dry-eyed, glad that I'd stopped by, ready to move on and out into a new chapter of my life.

23

YOU CAN'T TAKE IT WITH YOU, BUT YOU CAN SEND IT ON AHEAD

On Wednesday, August 26, 1981, friends and relatives came to formally show to one another their love and respect for Uncle. Aunt Dee, whom Uncle had brought to Portland along with my mother, came from Gig Harbor, Washington, along with her husband, Al Swanstrom. Uncle always referred to Al as 'the Swedish carpenter Ovidia married.' Uncle Johnny, my mother's brother, had come from Tacoma, accompanied by his wife, Arlene. Uncle had always spoken well of him, and it was interesting to have found in some of Uncle's personal effects, after his death, some cards and letters Johnny had sent to Uncle during WWII. Dick Peterson, Uncle's stepson, and his wife had come down from Seattle. Uncle and he had never been close, and Dick had been grown and pretty much out on his own when Uncle married his mother. Mick was there, still trucking along in spite of his inoperable brain tumor. The doctors are amazed how effective the radiation treatment has been. In fact, Mick assisted Uncle Johnny, Al, and several others as a pall bearer. Dawn, the young girl from our church who was such a comfort to Uncle during his last few days at the King City Care Center, was there with her camera. She was disappointed we had decided on a closed casket, for she thought an open one would have made a much better picture. I had asked our minister, Carl Blanchard, the one of "world's worst sermon" fame, if he'd mind offering a word of prayer during the service (after first clearing the idea with the Lutheran minister). The Millers from our church were there and, along with Ruth, Esther, Judi, Cathi, Berniece, a number of Uncle's neighbors, and a number of people from the Lutheran Church, quite a sizeable group of people had gathered.

The funeral service started with a hymn, followed by a greeting and invocation from the Lutheran Minister. The congregation participated in a reading. We listened to a vocal solo, and then I was introduced to read some scriptures and make (what those from the Lutheran church, who'd' never shared a funeral with a Baptist, hoped would be) appropriate remarks. I said, "I must say I sorrow not for Uncle. The debilities of extreme old age made the happy moments, and he had a lot of them, grow few and farther between. Uncle loved life and lived it to the fullest in the best possible sense." I then recounted to them an exchange of words several months earlier between Uncle and the minister of the very church we were having the service in. Uncle had told the minister that he was ready to die and couldn't understand why the Lord hadn't taken him yet. "Charlie," the minister replied, "you'll be taken when it's the Lord's time and not a moment before." I reminded them that that time had now come and gave a few more details of Uncle's death. I then moved into an explanation as to how Uncle fit into my life and that of my family and, going back as far as I could, reconstructed from birth to death some of the notable events in Uncle's life. I spent a considerable amount of time retelling many of the stories told earlier in this book. I ended with an account of one of our many luncheon meetings.

Uncle and I were at the Tyee in Tumwater for a luncheon meeting several months ago and Uncle preferred to eat his hamburger in the car. I went out and checked on him about every twenty to thirty minutes, and on about the third trip, to my surprise, I found Uncle crying. I scooted in next to him and asked what was the matter. Uncle, between sobs, said, "A hand grabbed me by the shoulder and a voice said, 'Charlie, your time is up!'" I asked him if he thought it was God. Uncle quickly responded, "It was a big hand, so it sure could have been!"

"God wasn't warning Uncle that time, but that dream must have come from a deep-seated desire to be absent from his body and face to face with the Lord. Uncle's wish to depart from a life greatly depleted by his almost completely diminished senses has now been realized. His own words, 'Oh, Lord, take me out of this mess!' (a phrase we heard when things weren't to his liking or because of his debilities) has now been realized. The Lord has taken him, and truly blessed in His eyes is the death of this saint."

Upon concluding my remarks, I introduced Pastor Blanchard, our "Church on the Prairie" minister, who offered a prayer. The Lutheran minister made some very appropriate remarks and the pronounced the benediction. The congregation sang one last hymn and all who so desired were given the opportunity to file past the closed casket. Then I, along with the minister, proceeded Uncle's casket down the aisle, into the foyer, and out through the massive front doors to the waiting hearse. Once the casket was in place and the doors shut, we got in our cars and lined up for the ride to the cemetery. A uniformed off-duty policeman led the way, and the funeral procession wound its way the several dozen blocks to the cemetery and graveside service.

The pall bearers carried Uncle's remains the final few feet to the prepared place beneath the large, leafy willow. The casket was placed on the stand, ready to be lowered into the earth by the cemetery grounds staff, to await resurrection next to Gertrude and the reuniting of their bodies with their departed souls and I closed the committal service with a word of prayer. The funeral director, to facilitate the awkward moments that always seem to follow this point, assisted the pall bearers in placing their boutonnieres on the casket and said, "This concludes the service for Mr. Ono. Stay as long as you would like."

We turned to one another and, after some embracing, chatted, looked over Gertrude and Uncle's headstone, noting that Uncle's grave was the last to be filled in that area. Finally, we walked back to our cars to drive back to the church, where the Lutheran ladies had prepared a very nice lunch. I waited briefly for the hearse parked directly in front of me, but since it didn't move, I eased around the long vehicle, having to go up on the cemetery grass a bit to get by. As I pulled even with the driver's window, he looked over, shrugged his shoulder, and said, "It's dead." Where Uncle was involved, the unexpected could be expected. It was almost as if Uncle had reached out one last time with some "funeral folly."

Half way through the delightful church luncheon, Ruth stood up and gave a short word of appreciation which ended with a vocal emotional quiver that left none doubting the sincerity of her gratitude.

We visited for a few minutes after the luncheon with some of the people who'd known Uncle and some of the ladies who had served us,

and then left for Ruth and Esther's. They, too, had prepared an array
of delicate goodies, and we all sat around visiting. Naturally, much of
the conversation involved Uncle. I had brought along a cassette tape
that Uncle and I had made, full of songs he'd sung and questions I'd
asked with Uncle's answers. It also included a few classic tales which
only could be told perfectly by Uncle himself. Evening had arrived
before we headed home from what truly had been a memorable
memorial to Uncle.

A couple of weeks later, I made my last trip to Uncle's grave. I've
never felt any strong compulsion to visit and decorate the grave sites of
those I love. I feel it's best to give to those you care about when you
both can enjoy the benefits together. For example, I feel good about
what I've been able to give Uncle while he was alive. He enjoyed our
many miles, appreciated my wife and daughters, basked in the bounty
of love and acceptance that permeates our home, and showed genuine
interest and concern for those we met together along the way. Now, as
I looked at the grave with its sunken sod, I could say with the Apostle
Paul, "Oh, death, where is your sting? O, grave, where is your
victory?"

AFTERWORD

Three weeks after Uncle's death, on an Indian summer afternoon, right after church, Joshua, our minister Carl's five-and-a-half-year-old son, invited himself home with us. Joshua is extremely bright, often baffling his doctoral candidate father with questions like, "Dad, can worms smile?" Well, this time he used his brightness to gain both his mother's and my approval at the same time.

As I stood talking to Dorothy, Carl's wife, Joshua bounced onto the scene, insinuated himself in between us, and with the skill of a seasoned director striking at the precise instant for achieving the desired effect, spoke the lines he must have carefully rehearsed just for this moment, "Mother, can I go home and spend the afternoon with Gary and Judi? Oh, please, Mother?"

Embarrassed only slightly, since for her this is a nearly every day occurrence, she rather abruptly replied, "Joshua, Gary and Judi didn't ask you and don't want you pestering them this afternoon!"

"Oh, yes, they do. Don't you, Gary?" Joshua looked at me, his deep, liquid blue eyes peering between ringlets of delightfully disordered sandy hair, and gave me his special smile, the one where the right side went up slightly higher into the cheek than the left. What could I say?

Joshua, Judi, the girls and I walked out and climbed into the '78 Volare that we'd driven to church earlier that morning. The girls got into the back seat and Judi and I in the front with Joshua in between. I started up the Volare, backed out of our parking spot, looped around the lone mercury lamppost in the center of our church's parking lot, and followed the part gravel and asphalt driveway to the county road. As we turned left onto the main road, I glanced over at Joshua to see how he was doing. His neck was craned; he was sniffing the air while at the same time looking in the back seat and all around him. At last he inquired, "Where's Uncle Charlie? I can smell him, but I thought he died."

Uncle indeed was gone but his "aroma" inside the '78 Volare, especially where Joshua was sitting on the front passenger seat, would linger indefinitely. The odor remained so strong that when the company got me a new car, the Volare's carpeting had to be completely stripped, the inside of the car cleaned to the metal, and new carpeting installed. But even these drastic measures didn't totally eliminate the odor. It took several months and several price reductions before someone came along, apparently with a smelling deficiency, and bought the car.

However, in a symbolic sense, the fragrance of Uncle's life also lingers on, providing us and many others with memories that will never be forgotten.

Recently, I asked Judi and my daughters five questions, some of which might have come to your mind as you read this book, pertaining to their individual reflections and attitudes towards Uncle and his sojourn with us. Here are the questions followed by each of their independent, written responses.

Question: What did the experience teach you?

Berniece: "Having Uncle Charlie live with us taught me lots of patience. Times when I became frustrated, I had to realize that Uncle was like a child (in some ways – dependant and helpless), and I needed to be the adult in the situation. Uncle also taught me many things about growing old. For example, these included good and bad things. Some good things were how we need to love people and respect and take care of them while they are alive. Another thing he taught me is how priceless our memories can be!"

Cathi: "Uncle taught me a great deal about being old. First of all, old age does not necessarily mean a life of boredom, depression, and isolation. Uncle enjoyed his life to the fullest, making the best of his infirmities. His example has been a great challenge – if he could make the best of life at ninety-eight, unable to hear, see or walk well, then so should I. After all, my troubles are hardly comparable to Uncle's."

Judi: "Uncle taught me patience and also a new perspective on life. Some of the things I was fretting over wouldn't really matter later. Uncle had endured numerous disappointments, hardships, etc., and yet life went on and here he was in his nineties and did it matter that he didn't do so well on a test, the car broke down, or some other trivial trial of daily living? No. This gave me perspective to value situations in my life that would carry through into my latter years and let go of the small stuff."

Question: What was most memorable?

Berniece: "Uncle Charlie's squeaky little voice singing his 'Daisy Bell' song."

Cathi: "I remember his darling appearance that characterized his unique personality. He was a cute little Norwegian man, rather plump, who always wore a little cap and gold, round-rimmed glasses. It makes me happy to reflect on these occasions when he sang an old song or told a joke. His twinkling eyes, jovial laughter, and warm smile would light up the whole room and everyone around him."

Judi: "What was most memorable to me was Uncle's smile and chuckle – his sense of humor."

Question: Would you be willing to do it again knowing what you know now? Explain.

Berniece: "I would be willing to have any older person in our home again. The things that I had to do were a small price to pay for the rewards I got! I learned so much about growing old, and now I feel I can better relate to other old people."

Cathi: "Yes, it was an opportunity to know and come to love a most unusual and interesting individual."

Judi: "Yes. Hard to explain, though – like explaining would I have my children knowing what I know now. Of course; they are a part of me – my life. Would I take in someone else? With this, there is some reservation; Uncle over again – absolutely."

Question: Do you have any negative feeling because of the inconvenience and sacrifices?

Berniece: "No – see question just before."

Cathi: "I have no negative feelings and if I did they are all resolved. I have realized that I have received far more in return for the little that I have given."

Judi: "No."

Question: What would you consider helpful for someone contemplating a similar care commitment:

Berniece: "Try and be as patient and understanding as possible. This attitude will be helpful for both parties. Do it out of love rather than grudgingly, doing it out of 'duty'."

Cathi: "In short, my advice is to look to I Corinthians 13. Without God's direction, it is hard to give love and care to elderly persons who, according to society, have nothing left to offer."

Judi: "What would I consider helpful?"

1. "To get their home physically set up, as much as possible, to accommodate the person. Adequate space, quarters, etc. Use convenient supplies – disposable chuxs, portable commodes, etc."

2. "To take time off from the situation and have someone else fill in for a few days."

3. "To carry on (as much as possible) with your life as usual."

4. "To hug, touch, look at, and talk with the person – make their last days be days of love, attention and support."

5. "Keep a sense of humor and perspective – 'someday, you'll (I'll) be old.'"

These words of comfort written to our family by some dear friends are a fitting close to this book:

Thinking of you these days and of the memory of the many wonderful stories, and our afternoon with Uncle Charlie. He must have given so much to your family, as your family gave to him – he was truly a unique and delightful man.

We feel very lucky to have met Uncle Charlie even briefly; for he is what life is all about. Families like yours are unique, too, and the strength amongst you is evident. What you were able to give to Uncle Charlie takes that special strength, and his memory for us will be one of a man having led a rich and full life being given the love and support to close the final chapter amongst those who care for and understand him. It has been beautiful to watch and hear about.

56526172R00134

Made in the USA
Columbia, SC
26 April 2019